John Stuart Mill

ON SOCIALISM
&
THE SUBJECTION
OF WOMEN

ON SOCIALISM
&
THE SUBJECTION
OF WOMEN

John Stuart Mill

Reprinted by Frederick Ellis
8000 E. Girard, Suite 507
Denver CO 80231

ISBN 978-0-9793363-2-5

ON SOCIALISM

Preliminary Notice

It was in the year 1869 that, impressed with the degree in which, even during the last twenty years, when the world seemed so wholly occupied with other matters, the socialist ideas of speculative thinkers had spread among the workers in every civilized country, Mr. Mill formed the design of writing a book on Socialism. Convinced that the inevitable tendencies of modern society must be to bring the questions involved in it always more and more to the front, he thought it of great practical consequence that they should be thoroughly and impartially considered, and the lines pointed out by which the best speculatively-tested theories might, without prolongation of suffering on the one hand, or unnecessary disturbance on the other, be applied to the existing order of things. He therefore planned a work which should go exhaustively through the whole subject, point by point; and the four chapters now printed are the first rough drafts thrown down towards the foundation of that work. These chapters might not, when the work came to be competely written out and then re-written, according to the author's habit, have appeared in the present order; they might have been incorporated into different parts of the work. It has not been without hesitation that I have yielded to the urgent wish of the editor of this Review to give these chapters to the world; but I have complied with his request because, while they appear to me to possess great intrinsic value as well as special application to the problems now forcing themselves on public attention, they will not, I believe, detract even from the mere literary reputation of their author, but will rather form an example of the patient labor with which good work is done.

HELEN TAYLOR

January, 1879

One

Introductory

In the great country beyond the Atlantic, which is now well-nigh the most powerful country in the world, and will soon be indisputably so, manhood suffrage prevails. Such is also the political qualification of France since 1848, and has become that of the German Confederation, though not of all the several states composing it. In Great Britain the suffrage is not yet so widely extended, but the last Reform Act admitted within what is called the pale of the Constitution so large a body of those who live on weekly wages, that as soon and as often as these shall choose to act together as a class, and exert for any common object the whole of the electoral power which our present institutions give them, they will exercise, though not a complete ascendancy, a very great influence on legislation. Now these are the very class which, in the vocabulary of the higher ranks, are said to have no stake in the country. Of course they have in reality the greatest stake, since their daily bread depends on its prosperity. But they are not engaged (we may call it bribed) by any peculiar interest of their own, to the support of property as it is, least of all to the support of inequalities of property. So far as their power reaches, or may hereafter reach, the laws of property have to depend for support upon considerations of a public nature, upon the estimate made of their conduciveness to the general welfare, and not upon motives of a mere personal character operating on the minds of those who have control over the Government.

It seems to me that the greatness of this change is as yet by no means completely realized, either by those who opposed, or by those who effected our last constitutional reform. To say the truth, the perceptions of Englishmen are of late somewhat blunted as to the tendencies of political changes. They have seen so many changes made, from which, while only in prospect, vast expectations were entertained, both of evil and of good, while the results of either kind that actually followed seemed far short of what had been predicted, that they have come to feel as if it were the nature of political changes not to fulfill expectation, and have fallen into a habit of half-unconscious belief that such changes, when they take place without a violent revolution, do not much or permanently disturb in practice the course of things habitual to the country. This, however, is but a superficial view either of the past or of the future. The various reforms of the last two generations have been at least as fruitful in important consequences as was foretold. The predictions were often erroneous as to the suddenness of the effects, and sometimes even as to the kind of effect. We laugh at the vain expectations of those who thought that Catholic emancipation would tranquilize Ireland, or reconcile it to British rule. At the end of the first ten years of the Reform Act of 1832, few continued to think either that it would remove every important practical grievance, or that it had opened the door to universal suffrage. But five-and-twenty years more of its operation have given scope for a large development of its indirect working, which is much more momentous than the direct. Sudden effects in history are generally superficial. Causes which go deep down into the roots of future events produce the most serious parts of their effect only slowly, and have, therefore, time to become a part of the familiar order of things before general attention is called to the changes they are producing; since, when the changes do become evident, they are often not seen, by cursory observers, to be in any peculiar manner connected with the cause. The remoter consequences of a new political fact are seldom understood when they occur, except when they have been appreciated beforehand.

This timely appreciation is particularly easy in respect to the tendencies of the change made in our institutions by the Reform Act of 1867. The great increase of electoral power which the Act places within the reach of the working classes is permanent. The circumstances which have caused them, thus far, to make a very limited use of that power, are essentially temporary. It is known even to the most inobservant, that the working classes have, and are likely to have, political objects which concern them as working classes, and on which they believe, rightly or wrongly, that the interests and opinions of the other powerful classes are opposed to theirs. However much their pursuit of these objects may be for the present retarded by want of electoral organization, by dissensions among themselves, or by their not having reduced as yet their wishes into a sufficiently definite practical shape, it is as certain as anything in politics can be, that they will before long find the means of making their collective electoral power effectively instrumental to the promotion of their collective objects. And when they do so, it will not be in the disorderly and ineffective way which belongs to a people not habituated to the use of legal and constitutional machinery, nor will it be by the impulse of a mere instinct of levelling. The instruments will be the press, public meetings and associations, and the return to Parliament of the greatest possible number of persons pledged to the political aims of the working classes. The political aims will themselves be determined by definite political doctrines; for politics are now scientifically studied from the point of view of the working classes, and opinions conceived in the special interest of those classes are organized into systems and creeds which lay claim to a place on the platform of political philosophy, by the same right as the systems elaborated by previous thinkers. It is of the utmost importance that all reflecting persons should take into early consideration what these popular political creeds are likely to be, and that every single article of them should be brought under the fullest light of investigation and discussion, so that, if possible, when the time shall be ripe, whatever is right in them may be adopted, and what is wrong rejected by general consent, and that instead of a hostile conflict, physical or only moral, between the old and the new, the best parts of both may be combined in a renovated social fabric. At the ordinary pace of those great social changes which are not effected by physical violence, we have before us an interval of about a generation, on the due employment of which it depends whether the accommodation of social institutions to the altered state of human society, shall be the work of wise foresight, or of a conflict of opposite prejudices. The future of mankind will be gravely imperilled, if great questions are left to be fought over between ignorant change and ignorant opposition to change.

And the discussion that is now required is one that must go down to the very first principles of existing society. The fundamental doctrines which were assumed as incontestable by former generations, are now put again on their trial. Until the present age, the institution of property in the shape in which it has been handed down from the past, had not, except by a few speculative writers, been brought seriously into question, because the conflicts of the past have always been conflicts between classes, both of which had a stake in the existing constitution of property. It will not be possible to go on longer in this manner. When the discussion includes classes who have next to no property of their own, and are only interested in the institution so far as it is a public benefit, they will not allow anything to be taken for granted—certainly not the principle of private property, the legitimacy and utility of which are denied by many of the reasoners who look out from the standpoint of the working classes. Those classes will certainly demand that the subject, in all its parts, shall be reconsidered from the foundation; that all proposals for doing without the institution, and all modes of

modifying it which have the appearance of being favorable
to the interest of the working classes, shall receive the fullest
consideration and discussion before it is decided that the
subject must remain as it is. As far as this country is concerned, the dispositions of the working classes have as yet
manifested themselves hostile only to certain outlying portions of the proprietary system. Many of them desire to
withdraw questions of wages from the freedom of contract,
which is one of the ordinary attributions of private property.
The more aspiring of them deny that land is a proper subject
for private appropriation, and have commenced an agitation
for its resumption by the State. With this is combined, in the
speeches of some of the agitators, a denunciation of what
they term usury, but without any definition of what they
mean by the name; and the cry does not seem to be of home
origin, but to have been caught up from the intercourse
which has recently commenced through the Labor Congresses and the International Society, with the continental
Socialists who object to all interest on money, and deny the
legitimacy of deriving an income in any form from property
apart from labor. This doctrine does not as yet show signs of
being widely prevalent in Great Britain, but the soil is well
prepared to receive the seeds of this description which are
widely scattered from those foreign countries where large,
general theories, and schemes of vast promise, instead of
inspiring distrust, are essential to the popularity of a cause.
It is in France, Germany, and Switzerland that anti-property
doctrines in the widest sense have drawn large bodies of
working men to rally round them. In these countries nearly
all those who aim at reforming society in the interest of the
working classes profess themselves Socialists, a designation

under which schemes of very diverse character are comprehended and confounded, but which implies at least a remodelling generally approaching to abolition of the institution of private property. And it would probably be found that even in England the more prominent and active leaders of the working classes are usually in their private creed Socialists of one order or another, though being, like most English politicians, better aware than their Continental brethren that great and permanent changes in the fundamental ideas of mankind are not to be accomplished by a *coup de main,* they direct their practical efforts towards ends which seem within easier reach, and are content to hold back all extreme theories until there has been experience of the operation of the same principles on a partial scale. While such continues to be the character of the English working classes, as it is of Englishmen in general, they are not likely to rush headlong into the reckless extremities of some of the foreign Socialists, who, even in sober Switzerland, proclaim themselves content to begin by simple subversion, leaving the subsequent reconstruction to take care of itself; and by subversion they mean not only the annihilation of all government, but getting all property of all kinds out of the hands of the possessors to be used for the general benefit; but in what mode it will, they say, be time enough afterwards to decide.

The avowal of this doctrine by a public newspaper, the organ of an association *(La Solidarité,* published at Neuchâtel), is one of the most curious signs of the times. The leaders of the English working men—whose delegates at the congresses of Geneva and Bâle contributed much the greatest part of such practical common sense as was shown there— are not likely to begin deliberately by anarchy, without having formed any opinion as to what form of society should be established in the room of the old. But it is evident that whatever they do propose can only be properly judged, and the grounds of the judgment made convincing to the general mind, on the basis of a previous survey of the two rival theories, that of private property and that of Socialism, one or other of which must necessarily furnish most of the premises in the discussion. Before, therefore, we can usefully discuss this class of questions in detail, it will be advisable to examine from their foundations the general questions raised by Socialism. And this examination should be made without any hostile prejudice. However irrefutable the arguments in favor of the laws of property may appear to those to whom they have the double prestige of immemorial custom and of personal interest, nothing is more natural than that a working man who has begun to speculate on politics, should regard them in a very different light. Having, after long struggles, attained in some countries, and nearly attained in others, the point at which for them, at least, there is no further progress to make in the department of purely political rights, is it possible that the less fortunate classes among the "adult males" should not ask themselves whether progress ought to stop there? Notwithstanding all that has been done, and all that seems likely to be done, in the extension of franchises, a few are born to great riches, and the many to penury, made only more grating by contrast. No longer enslaved or made dependent by force of law, the great majority are so by force of poverty; they are still chained to a place, to an occupation, and to conformity with the will of an employer, and debarred by the accident of birth both from the enjoyments, and from the mental and moral advantages, which others inherit without exertion and independently of desert. That this is an evil equal to almost any of those against which mankind have hitherto struggled, the poor are not wrong in believing. Is it a necessary evil? They are told so by those who do not feel it—by those who have gained the prizes in the lottery of life. But it was also said that slavery, that despotism, that all the privileges of oligarchy were necessary. All the successive steps that have been made by the poorer classes, partly won from the better feelings of the powerful, partly extorted from their fears, and partly bought with money, or attained in exchange for support given to one section of the powerful in its quarrels with another, had the strongest prejudices opposed to them beforehand; but their acquisition was a sign of power gained by the subordinate classes, a means to those classes of acquiring more; it consequently drew to those classes a certain share of the respect accorded to power, and produced a corresponding modification in the creed of society respecting them; whatever advantages they succeeded in acquiring came to be considered their due, while, of those which they had not yet attained, they continued to be deemed unworthy. The classes, therefore, which the system of society makes subordinate, have little reason to put faith in any of the maxims which the same system of society may have established as principles. Considering that the opinions of mankind have been found so wonderfully flexible, have always tended to consecrate existing facts, and to declare what did not yet exist, either pernicious or impracticable, what assurance have those classes that the distinction of rich and poor is grounded on a more imperative necessity than those other ancient and long-established facts, which, having been abolished, are now condemned even by those who formerly profited by them? This cannot be taken on the word of an interested party. The working classes are entitled to claim that the whole field of social institutions should be reexamined, and every question considered as if it now arose for the first time; with the idea constantly in view that the persons who are to be convinced are not those who owe their ease and importance to the present system, but persons who have no other interest in the matter than abstract justice and the general good of the community. It should be the object to acertain what institutions of property would be established by an unprejudiced legislator, absolutely impartial between the possessors of property and the nonpossessors; and to defend and justify them by the reasons which would really influence such a legislator, and not by such as have the appearance of being got up to make out a case for what already exists. Such rights or privileges of property as will not stand this test will, sooner or later, have to be given up. An impartial hearing ought, moreover, to be given to all objections against property itself. All evils and inconveniences attaching to the institution in its best form ought to be frankly admitted, and the best remedies or palliatives applied which human intelligence is able to devise. And all plans proposed by social reformers, under whatever name designated, for the purpose of attaining the benefits aimed at by the institution of property without its inconveniences, should be examined with the same candor, not prejudged as absurd or impracticable.

Two

Socialist Objections to the Present Order of Society

As in all proposals for change there are two elements to be considered—that which is to be changed, and that which it is to be changed to—so in Socialism considered generally, and in each of its varieties taken separately, there are two parts to be distinguished, the one negative and critical, the other constructive. There is, first, the judgment of Socialism on existing institutions and practices and on their results; and secondly, the various plans which it has propounded for doing better. In the former all the different schools of Socialism are at one. They agree almost to identity in the faults which they find with the economical order of existing society. Up to a certain point also they entertain the same general conception of the remedy to be provided for those faults; but in the details, notwithstanding this general agreement, there is a wide disparity. It will be both natural and convenient, in attempting an estimate of their doctrines, to begin with the negative portion which is common to them all, and to postpone all mention of their differences until we arrive at that second part of their undertaking, in which alone they seriously differ.

This first part of our task is by no means difficult; since it consists only in an enumeration of existing evils. Of these there is no scarcity, and most of them are by no means obscure or mysterious. Many of them are the veriest commonplaces of moralists, though the roots even of these lie deeper than moralists usually attempt to penetrate. So various are they that the only difficulty is to make any approach to an exhaustive catalogue. We shall content ourselves for the present with mentioning a few of the principal. And let one thing be remembered by the reader. When item after item of the enumeration passes before him, and he finds one fact after another which he has been accustomed to include among the necessities of nature urged as an accusation against social institutions, he is not entitled to cry unfairness, and to protest that the evils complained of are inherent in Man and Society, and are such as no arrangements can remedy. To assert this would be to beg the very question at issue. No one is more ready than Socialists to admit—they affirm it indeed much more decidedly than truth warrants—that the evils they complain of are irremediable in the present constitution of society. They propose to consider whether some other form of society may be devised which would not be liable to those evils, or would be liable to them in a much less degree. Those who object to the present order of society, considered as a whole, and who accept as an alternative the possibility of a total change, have a right to set down all the evils which at present exist in society as part of their case, whether these are apparently attributable to social arrangements or not, provided they do not flow from physical laws which human power is not adequate, or human knowledge has not yet learned, to counteract. Moral evils, and such physical evils as would be remedied if all persons did as they ought, are fairly chargeable against the state of society which admits of them; and are valid as arguments until it is shown that any other state of society would involve an equal or greater amount of such evils. In the opinion of Socialists, the present arrangements of society in respect to Property and the Production and Distribution of Wealth, are, as means to the general good, a total failure. They say that there is an enormous mass of evil which these arrangements do not succeed in preventing; that the good, either moral or physical, which they realize is wretchedly small compared with the amount of exertion employed, and that even this small amount of good is brought about by means which are full of pernicious consequences, moral and physical.

First among existing social evils may be mentioned the evil of Poverty. The institution of Property is upheld and commended principally as being the means by which labor and frugality are insured their reward, and mankind enabled to emerge from indigence. It may be so; most Socialists allow that it has been so in earlier periods of history. But if the institution can do nothing more or better in this respect than it has hitherto done, its capabilities, they affirm, are very insignificant. What proportion of the population, in the most civilized countries of Europe, enjoy in their own persons anything worth naming of the benefits of property? It may be said, that but for property in the hands of their employers they would be without daily bread; but, though this be conceded, at least their daily bread is all that they have; and that often in insufficient quantity; almost always of inferior quality; and with no assurance of continuing to have it at all; an immense proportion of the industrious classes being at some period or other of their lives (and all being liable to become) dependent, at least temporarily, on legal or voluntary charity. Any attempt to depict the miseries of indigence, or to estimate the proportion of mankind who in the most advanced countries are habitually given up during their whole existence to its physical and moral sufferings, would be superfluous here. This may be left to philanthropists, who have painted these miseries in colors sufficiently strong. Suffice it to say that the condition of numbers in civilized Europe, and even in England and France, is more wretched than that of most tribes of savages who are known to us.

It may be said that of this hard lot no one has any reason to complain, because it befalls those only who are outstripped by others, from inferiority of energy or of prudence. This, even were it true, would be a very small alleviation of the evil. If some Nero or Domitian were to require a hundred persons to run a race for their lives, on condition that the fifty or twenty who came in hindmost should be put to death, it would not be any diminution of the injustice that the strongest or nimblest would, except through some untoward accident, be certain to escape. The misery and the crime would be that any were put to death at all. So in the economy of society; if there be any who suffer physical privation or moral degradation, whose bodily necessities are either not satisfied or satisfied in a manner which only brutish creatures can be content with, this, though not necessarily the crime of society, is *pro tanto* a failure of the social arrangements. And to assert as a mitigation of the evil that those who thus suffer are the weaker members of the community, morally or physically, is to add insult to misfortune. Is weakness a justification of suffering? Is it not, on the contrary, an irresistible claim upon every human being for protection against suffering? If the minds and feelings of the prosperous were in a right state, would they accept their prosperity if for the sake of it even one person near them was, for any other cause than voluntary fault, excluded from obtaining a desirable existence?

One thing there is, which if it could be affirmed truly, would relieve social institutions from any share in the responsibility of these evils. Since the human race has no means of enjoyable existence, or of existence at all, but what it derives from its own labor and abstinence, there would be no ground for complaint against society if every one who was willing to undergo a fair share of this labor and abstinence could attain a fair share of the fruits. But is this the fact? Is it not the reverse of the fact? The reward, instead of being proportioned to the labor and abstinence of the individual, is almost in an inverse ratio to it: those who receive the least, labor and abstain the most. Even the idle, reckless, and ill-conducted poor, those who are said with most justice to have themselves to blame for their condition, often undergo much more and severer labor, not only than those

who are born to pecuniary independence, but than almost
any of the more highly remunerated of those who earn their
subsistence; and even the inadequate self-control exercised
by the industrious poor costs them more sacrifice and more
effort than is almost ever required from the more favored
members of society. The very idea of distributive justice, or
of any proportionality between success and merit, or between
success and exertion, is in the present state of society so
manifestly chimerical as to be relegated to the regions of
romance. It is true that the lot of individuals is not wholly
independent of their virtue and intelligence; these do really
tell in their favor, but far less than many other things in
which there is no merit at all. The most powerful of all the
determining circumstances is birth. The great majority are
what they were born to be. Some are born rich without
work, others are born to a position in which they can become rich *by* work, the great majority are born to hard
work and poverty throughout life, numbers to indigence.
Next to birth the chief cause of success in life is accident and
opportunity. When a person not born to riches succeeds in
acquiring them, his own industry and dexterity have generally contributed to the result; but industry and dexterity
would not have sufficed unless there had also been a concurrence of occasions and chances which falls to the lot of only
a small number. If persons are helped in their worldly career
by their virtues, so are they, and perhaps quite as often, by
their vices: by servility and sycophancy, by hard-hearted and
close-fisted selfishness, by the permitted lies and tricks of
trade, by gambling speculations, not seldom by downright
knavery. Energies and talents are of much more avail for
success in life than virtues; but if one man succeeds by em-

ploying energy and talent in something generally useful, another thrives by exercising the same qualities in out-generaling and ruining a rival. It is as much as any moralist ventures to assert, that, other circumstances being given, honesty is the best policy, and that with parity of advantages an honest person has better chances than a rogue. Even this in many stations and circumstances of life is questionable; anything more than this is out of the question. It cannot be pretended that honesty, as a means of success, tells for as much as a difference of one single step on the social ladder. The connection between fortune and conduct is mainly this, that there is a degree of bad conduct, or rather of some kinds of bad conduct, which suffices to ruin any amount of good fortune; but the converse is not true: in the situation of most people no degree whatever of good conduct can be counted upon for raising them in the world, without the aid of fortunate accidents.

These evils, then—great poverty, and that poverty very little connected with desert—are the first grand failure of the existing arrangements of society. The second is human misconduct; crime, vice, and folly, with all the sufferings which follow in their train. For, nearly all the forms of misconduct, whether committed towards ourselves or towards others, may be traced to one of three causes: Poverty and its temptations in the many; Idleness and *désoeuvrement* in the few whose circumstances do not compel them to work; bad education, or want of education, in both. The first two must be allowed to be at least failures in the social arrangements, the last is now almost universally admitted to be the fault of those arrangements—it may almost be said the crime. I am speaking loosely and in the rough, for a minuter analysis of the sources of faults of character and errors of conduct would establish far more conclusively the filiation which connects them with a defective organization of society, though it would also show the reciprocal dependence of that faulty state of society on a backward state of the human mind.

At this point, in the enumeration of the evils of society, the mere levellers of former times usually stopped: but their more farsighted successors, the present Socialists, go farther. In their eyes the very foundation of human life as at present constituted, the very principle on which the production and repartition of all material products is now carried on, is essentially vicious and anti-social. It is the principle of individualism, competition, each one for himself and against all the rest. It is grounded on opposition of interests, not harmony of interests, and under it every one is required to find his place by a struggle, by pushing others back or being pushed back by them. Socialists consider this system of private war (as it may be termed) between every one and every one, especially fatal in an economical point of view and in a moral. Morally considered, its evils are obvious. It is the parent of envy, hatred, and all uncharitableness; it makes every one the natural enemy of all others who cross his path, and every one's path is constantly liable to be crossed. Under the present system hardly any one can gain except by the loss or disappointment of one or of many others. In a well-constituted community every one would be a gainer by every other person's successful exertions; while now we gain by each other's loss and lose by each other's gain, and our greatest gains come from the worst source of all, from death, the death of those who are nearest and should be dearest to us. In its purely economical operation the principle of individual competition receives an unqualified condemnation from the social reformers as in its moral. In the competition of laborers they see the cause of low wages; in the competition of producers the cause of ruin and bankruptcy; and both evils, they affirm, tend constantly to increase as population and wealth make progress; no person (they conceive) being benefited except the great proprietors of land, the holders of fixed money incomes, and a few great capitalists, whose wealth is gradually enabling them to undersell all other producers, to absorb the whole of the operations of industry into their own sphere, to drive from the market all employers of labor except themselves, and to convert the laborers into a kind of slaves or serfs, dependent on them for the means of support, and compelled to accept these on such terms as they choose to offer. Society, in short, is travelling onward, according to these speculators, towards a new feudality, that of the great capitalists.

As I shall have ample opportunity in future chapters to state my own opinion on these topics, and on many others connected with and subordinate to them, I shall now, without further preamble, exhibit the opinions of distinguished Socialists on the present arrangements of society, in a selection of passages from their published writings. For the present I desire to be considered as a mere reporter of the opinions of others. Hereafter it will appear how much of what I cite agrees or differs with my own sentiments.

The clearest, the most compact, and the most precise and specific statement of the case of the Socialists generally against the existing order of society in the economical department of human affairs, is to be found in the little work of M. Louis Blanc, *Organisation du Travail* [*The Organi-*

zation of Labor]. My first extracts, therefore, on this part of
the subject, shall be taken from that treatise.

Competition is for the people a system of extermina-
tion. Is the poor man a member of society, or an enemy
to it? We ask for an answer.

All around him he finds the soil preoccupied. Can he
cultivate the earth for himself? No; for the right of the
first occupant has become a right of property. Can he
gather the fruits which the hand of God ripens on the
path of man? No; for, like the soil, the fruits have been
appropriated. Can he hunt or fish? No; for that is a right
which is dependent upon the government. Can he draw
water from a spring enclosed in a field? No; for the proprietor of the field is, in virtue of his right to the field,
proprietor of the fountain. Can he, dying of hunger and
thirst, stretch out his hands for the charity of his fellow-
creatures? No; for there are laws against begging. Can he,
exhausted by fatigue and without a refuge, lie down to
sleep upon the pavement of the streets? No; for there are
laws against vagabondage. Can he, flying from the cruel
native land where everything is denied him, seek the
means of living far from the place where life was given
him? No; for it is not permitted to change your country
except on certain conditions which the poor man cannot
fulfill.

What, then, can the unhappy man do? He will say, "I
have hands to work with, I have intelligence, I have
youth, I have strength; take all this, and in return give me
a morsel of bread." This is what the working men do say.
But even here the poor man may be answered, "I have no
work to give you." What is he to do then?

*   *   *   *   *   *

What is competition from the point of view of the workman? It is work put up to auction. A contractor wants a workman: three present themselves.—How much for your work?—Half-a-crown: I have a wife and children.—Well; and how much for yours?—Two shillings: I have no children, but I have a wife.—Very well; and now how much for you?—One and eightpence are enough for me; I am single. Then you shall have the work. It is done; the bargain is struck. And what are the other two workmen to do? It is to be hoped they will die quietly of hunger. But what if they take to thieving? Never fear; we have the police. To murder? We have got the hangman. As for the lucky one, his triumph is only temporary. Let a fourth workman make his appearance, strong enough to fast every other day, and his price will run down still lower; then there will be a new outcast, a new recruit for the prison perhaps!

Will it be said that these melancholy results are exaggerated; that at all events they are only possible when there is not enough work for the hands that seek employment? But I ask, in answer, Does the principle of competition contain, by chance, within itself any method by which this murderous disproportion is to be avoided? If one branch of industry is in want of hands, who can answer for it that, in the confusion created by universal competition, another is not overstocked? And if, out of thirty-four millions of men, twenty are really reduced to theft for a living, this would suffice to condemn the principle.

But who is so blind as not to see that under the system of unlimited competition, the continual fall of wages is no exceptional circumstance, but a necessary and general fact? Has the population a limit which it cannot exceed? Is it possible for us to say to industry—

industry given up to the accidents of individual egotism and fertile in ruin—can we say, "Thus far shalt thou go, and no farther?" The population increases constantly: tell the poor mother to become sterile, and blaspheme the God who made her fruitful, for if you do not the lists will soon become too narrow for the combatants. A machine is invented: command it to be broken, and anathematize science, for if you do not, the thousand workmen whom the new machine deprives of work will knock at the door of the neighboring workshop, and lower the wages of their companions. Thus systematic lowering of wages, ending in the driving out of a certain number of workmen, is the inevitable effect of unlimited competition. It is an industrial system by means of which the working classes are forced to exterminate one another.

*   *   *   *   *   *

If there is an undoubted fact, it is that the increase of population is much more rapid among the poor than among the rich. According to the *Statistics of European Population,* the births at Paris are only one-thirty-second of the population in the rich quarters, while in the others they rise to one-twenty-sixth. This disproportion is a general fact, and M. de Sismondi, in his work on Political Economy, has explained it by the impossibility for the workmen of hopeful prudence. Those only who feel themselves assured of the morrow can regulate the number of their children according to their income; he who lives from day to day is under the yoke of a mysterious fatality, to which he sacrifices his children as he was sacri-

ficed to it himself. It is true the workhouses exist, menac-
ing society with an inundation of beggars—what way is
there of escaping from the cause? . . . It is clear that any
society where the means of subsistence increase less rapidly than the numbers of the population, is a society on
the brink of an abyss . . . . Competition produces destitution; this is a fact shown by statistics. Destitution is
fearfully prolific; this is shown by statistics. The fruit-
fulness of the poor throws upon society unhappy creatures who have the need of work and cannot find it; this
is shown by statistics. At this point society is reduced to a
choice between killing the poor or maintaining them gra-
tuitously—between atrocity or folly.[1]

So much for the poor. We now pass to the middle
classes.

According to the political economists of the school
of Adam Smith and Léon Say, *cheapness* is the word in
which may be summed up the advantages of unlimited
competition. But why persist in considering the effect of
cheapness with a view only to the momentary advantage
of the consumer? Cheapness is advantageous to the consumer at the cost of introducing the seeds of ruinous
anarchy among the producers. Cheapness is, so to speak,
the hammer with which the rich among the producers
crush their poorer rivals. Cheapness is the trap into which
the daring speculators entice the hard-workers. Cheapness
is the sentence of death to the producer on a small scale
who has no money to invest in the purchase of machinery
that his rich rivals can easily procure. Cheapness is the

great instrument in the hands of monopoly; it absorbs the
small manufacturer, the small shopkeeper, the small proprietor; it is, in one word, the destruction of the middle
classes for the advantage of a few industrial oligarchs.

Ought we, then, to consider cheapness as a curse? No
one would attempt to maintain such an absurdity. But it
is the speciality of wrong principles to turn good into evil
and to corrupt all things. Under the system of competition cheapness is only a provisional and fallacious advantage. It is maintained only so long as there is a struggle;
no sooner have the rich competitors driven out their
poorer rivals than prices rise. Competition leads to
monopoly, for the same reason cheapness leads to high
prices. Thus, what has been made use of as a weapon in
the contest between the producers, sooner or later becomes a cause of impoverishment among the consumers.
And if to this cause we add the others we have already
enumerated, first among which must be ranked the inor-
dinate increase of the population, we shall be compelled
to recognize the impoverishment of the mass of the consumers as a direct consequence of competition.

But, on the other hand, this very competition which
tends to dry up the sources of demand, urges production
to over-supply. The confusion produced by the universal
struggle prevents each producer from knowing the state
of the market. He must work in the dark and trust to
chance for a sale. Why should he check the supply, especially as he can throw any loss on the workman whose
wages are so preeminently liable to rise and fall? Even
when production is carried on at a loss the manufacturers
still often carry it on, because they will not let their machinery, &c., stand idle, or risk the loss of raw material,
or lose their customers; and because productive industry
as carried on under the competitive system being nothing

less than a game of chance, the gambler will not lose his chance of a lucky stroke.

Thus, and we cannot too often insist upon it, competition necessarily tends to increase supply and to diminish consumption; its tendency therefore is precisely the opposite of what is sought by economic science; hence it is not merely oppressive but foolish as well.

*   *   *   *   *   *

And in all this, in order to avoid dwelling on truths which have become commonplaces and sound declamatory from their very truth, we have said nothing of the frightful moral corruption which industry, organized, or more properly speaking disorganized as it is at the present day, has introduced among the middle classes. Everything has become venal, and competition invades even the domain of thought.

The factory crushing the workshop; the showy establishment absorbing the humble shop; the artisan who is his own master replaced by the day-laborer; cultivation by the plough superseding that by the spade, and bringing the poor man's field under disgraceful homage to the money-lender; bankruptcies multiplied; manufacturing industry transformed by the ill-regulated extension of credit into a system of gambling where no one, not even the rogue, can be sure of winning; in short a vast confusion calculated to arouse jealousy, mistrust, and hatred, and to stifle, little by little, all generous aspirations, all faith, self-sacrifice, and poetry—such is the hideous but only too faithful picture of the results obtained by the application of the principle of competition.[2]

The Fourierists, through their principal organ, M. Considérant, enumerate the evils of the existing civilization in the following order:

1. It employs an enormous quantity of labor and of human power unproductively, or in the work of destruction.

In the first place there is the army, which in France, as in all other countries, absorbs the healthiest and strongest men, a large number of the most talented and intelligent, and a considerable part of the public revenue. . . . The existing state of society develops in its impure atmosphere innumerable outcasts, whose labor is not merely unproductive, but actually destructive: adventurers, prostitutes, people with no acknowledged means of living, beggars, convicts, swindlers, thieves, and others whose number tends rather to increase than to diminish. . . .

To the list of unproductive labor fostered by our state of Society must be added that of the judicature and of the bar, of the courts and magistrates, the police, gaolers, executioners, &c.—functions indispensable to the state of society as it is.

Also people of what is called "good society"; those who pass their lives in doing nothing; idlers of all ranks.

Also the numberless custom-house officials, tax-gatherers, bailiffs, excisemen; in short, all that army of men which overlooks, brings to account, takes, but produces nothing.

Also the labors of sophists, philosophers, metaphysicians, political men, working in mistaken directions, who do nothing to advance science, and produce nothing but disturbance and sterile discussions; the verbiage of advocates, pleaders, witnesses, &c.

And finally all the operations of commerce, from those of the bankers and brokers, down to those of the grocer behind his counter.[3]

Secondly, they assert that even the industry and powers which in the present system are devoted to production, do not produce more than a small portion of what they might produce if better employed and directed:

> Who with any good-will and reflection will not see how much the want of coherence—the disorder, the want of combination, the parcelling out of labor and leaving it wholly to individual action without any organization, without any large or general views—are causes which limit the possibilities of production and destroy, or at least waste, our means of action? Does not disorder give birth to poverty, as order and good management give birth to riches? Is not want of combination a source of weakness, as combination is a source of strength? And who can say that industry, whether agricultural, domestic, manufacturing, scientific, artistic, or commercial, is organized at the present day either in the state or in municipalities? Who can say that all the work which is carried on in any of these departments is executed in subordination to any general views, or with foresight, economy, and order? Or, again, who can say that it is possible in our present state of society to develop, by a good education, all the faculties bestowed by nature on each of its members; to employ each one in functions which he would like, which he would be the most capable of, and

which, therefore, he could carry on with the greatest advantage to himself and to others? Has it even been so much as attempted to solve the problems presented by varieties of character so as to regulate and harmonize the varieties of employments in accordance with natural aptitudes? Alas! The Utopia of the most ardent philanthropists is to teach reading and writing to twenty-five millions of the French people! And in the present state of things we may defy them to succeed even in that!

And is it not a strange spectacle, too, and one which cries out in condemnation of us, to see this state of society where the soil is badly cultivated, and sometimes not cultivated at all; where man is ill lodged, ill clothed, and yet where whole masses are continually in need of work, and pining in misery because they cannot find it? Of a truth we are forced to acknowledge that if the nations are poor and starving it is not because nature has denied the means of producing wealth, but because of the anarchy and disorder in our employment of those means; in other words, it is because society is wretchedly constituted and labor unorganized.

But this is not all, and you will have but a faint conception of the evil if you do not consider that to all these vices of society, which dry up the sources of wealth and prosperity, must be added the struggle, the discord, the war, in short, under many names and many forms which society cherishes and cultivates between the individuals that compose it. These struggles and discords correspond to radical oppositions—deep-seated antinomies between the various interests. Exactly in so far as you are able to establish classes and categories within the nation; in so far, also, you will have opposition of interests and internal warfare either avowed or secret, even if you take into consideration the industrial system only.[4]

One of the leading ideas of this school is the wastefulness and at the same time the immorality of the existing arrangements for distributing the produce of the country among the various consumers, the enormous superfluity in point of number of the agents of distribution, the merchants, dealers, shopkeepers and their innumerable employees, and the depraving character of such a distribution of occupations.

It is evident that the interest of the trader is opposed to that of the consumer and of the producer. Has he not bought cheap and undervalued as much as possible in all his dealings with the producer, the very same article which, vaunting its excellence, he sells to you as dear as he can? Thus the interest of the commercial body, collectively and individually, is contrary to that of the producer and of the consumer—that is to say, to the interest of the whole body of society.

*   *   *   *   *   *

The trader is a go-between, who profits by the general anarchy and the nonorganization of industry. The trader buys up products, he buys up everything; he owns and detains everything, in such sort that:

1stly. He holds both Production and Consumption *under his yoke,* because both must come to him either finally for the products to be consumed, or at first for the raw materials to be worked up, Commerce with all its methods of buying, and of raising and lowering prices, its innumerable devices, and its holding everything in the

hands of *middle-men,* levies toll right and left: it des-
potically gives the law to Production and Consumption,
of which it ought to be only the subordinate.

2ndly. It robs society by its *enormous profits*—profits
levied upon the consumer and the producer, and altogether out of proportion to the services rendered, for
which a twentieth of the persons actually employed would
be sufficient.

3rdly. It robs society by the subtraction of its productive forces; taking off from productive labor nineteen-
twentieths of the agents of trade who are mere parasites.
Thus, not only does commerce rob society by appropri-
ating an exorbitant share of the common wealth, but also
by considerably diminishing the productive energy of the
human beehive. The great majority of traders would return to productive work if a rational system of commercial organization were substituted for the inextricable
chaos of the present state of things.

4thly. It robs society by the *adulteration* of products,
pushed at the present day beyond all bounds. And in
fact, if a hundred grocers establish themselves in a town
where before there were only twenty, it is plain that people will not begin to consume five times as many gro-
ceries. Hereupon the hundred virtuous grocers have to
dispute between them the profits which before were honestly made by the twenty; competition obliges them to
make it up at the expense of the consumer, either by
raising the prices as sometimes happens, or by adulterat-
ing the goods as always happens. In such a state of things
there is an end to good faith. Inferior or adulterated
goods are sold for articles of good quality whenever the
credulous customer is not too experienced to be deceived.
And when the customer has been thoroughly imposed
upon, the trading conscience consoles itself by saying, "I

state my price; people can take or leave; no one is obliged to buy." The losses imposed on the consumers by the bad quality or the adulteration of goods are incalculable.

5thly. It robs society by *accumulations,* artificial or not, in consequence of which vast quantities of goods, collected in one place, are damaged and destroyed for want of a sale. Fourier (Th. des Quat. Mouv., p. 334, 1st ed.) says: "The fundamental principle of the commercial systems, that of *leaving full liberty to the merchants,* gives them absolute right of property over the goods in which they deal; they have the right to withdraw them altogether, to withhold or even to burn them, as happened more than once with the Oriental Company of Amsterdam, which publicly burnt stores of cinnamon in order to raise the price. What it did with cinnamon it would have done with corn; but for the fear of being stoned by the populace, it would have burnt some corn in order to sell the rest at four times its value. Indeed, it actually is of daily occurrence in ports, for provisions of grains to be thrown into the sea because the merchants have allowed them to rot while waiting for a rise. I myself, when I was a clerk, have had to superintend these infamous proceedings, and in one day caused to be thrown into the sea some forty thousand bushels of rice, which might have been sold at a fair profit had the withholder been less greedy of gain. It is society that bears the cost of this waste, which takes place daily under shelter of the philosophical maxim of *full liberty for the merchants."*

6thly. Commerce robs society, moreover, by all the loss, damage, and waste that follows from the extreme scattering of products in millions of shops, and by the multiplication and complication of carriage.

7thly. It robs society by shameless and unlimited

usury—usury absolutely appalling. The trader carries on operations with fictitious capital, much higher in amount than his real capital. A trader with a capital of twelve hundred pounds will carry on operations, by means of bills and credit, on a scale of four, eight, or twelve thousand pounds. Thus he draws from capital *which he does not possess,* usurious interest, out of all proportion with the capital he actually owns.

8thly. It robs society by innumerable *bankruptcies,* for the daily accidents of our commercial system, political events, and any kind of disturbance, must usher in a day when the trader, having incurred obligations beyond his means, is no longer able to meet them; his failure, whether fraudulent or not, must be a severe blow to his creditors. The bankruptcy of some entails that of others, so that bankruptcies follow one upon another, causing widespread ruin. And it is always the producer and the consumer who suffer; for commerce, considered as a whole, does not produce wealth, and invests very little in proportion to the wealth which passes through its hands. How many are the manufactures crushed by these blows! how many fertile sources of wealth dried up by these devices, with all their disastrous consequences!

The producer furnishes the goods, the consumer the money. Trade furnishes credit, founded on little or no actual capital, and the different members of the commercial body are in no way responsible for one another. This, in a few words, is the whole theory of the thing.

9thly. Commerce robs society by the *independence* and *irresponsibility* which permits it to buy at the epochs when the producers are forced to sell and compete with one another, in order to procure money for their rent and necessary expenses of production. When the markets are overstocked and goods cheap, trade purchases. Then it creates a rise, and by this simple maneuver despoils both producer and consumer.

10thly. It robs society by a considerable *drawing off* of *capital,* which will return to productive industry when commerce plays its proper subordinate part, and is only an agency carrying on transactions between the producers (more or less distant) and the great centers of consumption—the communistic societies. Thus the capital engaged in the speculations of commerce (which, small as it is, compared to the immense wealth which passes through its hands, consists nevertheless of sums enormous in themselves), would return to stimulate production if commerce was deprived of the intermediate property in goods, and their distribution became a matter of administrative organization. Stock-jobbing is the most odious form of this vice of commerce.

11thly. It robs society by the *monopolizing* or buying up of raw materials. "For" (says Fourier, Th. des Quat. Mouv., p. 359, 1st ed.), "the rise in price on articles that are bought up, is borne ultimately by the consumer, although in the first place by the manufacturers, who, being obliged to keep up their establishments, must make pecuniary sacrifices, and manufacture at small profits in the hope of better days; and it is often long before they can repay themselves the rise in prices which the monopolizer has compelled them to support in the first instance. . . ."

In short, all these vices, besides many others which I omit, are multiplied by the extreme complication of mercantile affairs; for products do not pass once only through the greedy clutches of commerce; there are some which pass and repass twenty or thirty times before reaching the consumer. In the first place, the raw material passes through the grasp of commerce before reaching the manufacturer who first works it up; then it returns to com-

merce to be sent out again to be worked up in a second
form; and so on until it receives its final shape. Then it
passes into the hands of merchants, who sell to the wholesale dealers, and these to the great retail dealers of towns,
and these again to the little dealers and to the country
shops; and each time that it changes hands, it leaves
something behind it.

. . . One of my friends who was lately exploring the
Jura, where much working in metal is done, had occasion
to enter the house of a peasant who was a manufacturer
of shovels. He asked the price. "Let us come to an understanding," answered the poor laborer, not an economist at
all, but a man of common sense; "I sell them for 8*d*. to
the trade, which retails them at 1*s*. 8*d*. in the towns. If
you could find a means of opening a direct communica-
tion between the workman and the consumer, you might
have them for 1*s*. 2*d*., and we should each gain 6*d*. by the
transaction."[5]

To a similar effect Owen, in the *Book of the New Moral
World,* part 2, chap. iii.

The principle now in practice is to induce a large
portion of society to devote their lives to distribute wealth
upon a large, a medium, and a small scale, and to have it
conveyed from place to place in larger or smaller quantities, to meet the means and wants of various divisions of
society and individuals, as they are now situated in cities,
towns, villages, and country places. This principle of distribution makes a class in society whose business it is to
buy from some parties and to *sell to* others. By this

proceeding they are placed under circumstances which induce them to endeavor to buy at what appears at the time a low price in the market, and to sell again at the greatest permanent profit which they can obtain. Their real object being to get as much profit as gain between the seller to, and the buyer from them, as can be effected in their transactions.

There are innumerable errors in principle and evils in practice which necessarily proceed from this mode of distributing the wealth of society.

1st. A general class of distributors is formed, whose interest is separated from, and apparently opposed to, that of the individual from whom they buy and to whom they sell.

2nd. Three classes of distributors are made, the small, the medium, and the large buyers and sellers; or the retailers, the wholesale dealers, and the extensive merchants.

3rd. Three classes of buyers thus created constitute the small, the medium, and the large purchasers.

By this arrangement into various classes of buyers and sellers, the parties are easily trained to learn that they have separate and opposing interests, and different ranks and stations in society. An inequality of feeling and condition is thus created and maintained, with all the servility and pride which these unequal arrangements are sure to produce. The parties are regularly trained in a general system of deception, in order that they may be the more successful in buying cheap and selling dear.

The smaller sellers acquire habits of injurious idleness, waiting often for hours for customers. And this evil is experienced to a considerable extent even amongst the class of wholesale dealers.

There are, also, by this arrangement, many more establishments for selling than are necessary in the villages, towns, and cities; and a very large capital is thus wasted without benefit to society. And from their number opposed to each other all over the country to obtain customers, they endeavor to undersell each other, and are therefore continually endeavoring to injure the producer by the establishment of what are called cheap shops and warehouses; and to support their character the master of his servants must be continually on the watch to buy bargains, that is, to procure wealth for less than the cost of its production.

The distributors, small, medium, and large, have all to be supported by the producers, and the greater the number of the former compared with the latter, the greater will be the burden which the producer has to sustain; for as the number of distributors increases, the accumulation of wealth must decrease, and more must be required from the producer.

The distributors of wealth, under the present system, are a dead weight upon the producers, and are most active demoralizers of society. Their dependent condition, at the commencement of their task, teaches or induces them to be servile to their customers, and to continue to be so as long as they are accumulating wealth by their cheap buying and dear selling. But when they have secured sufficient to be what they imagine to be an independence—to live without business—they are too often filled with a most ignorant pride, and become insolent to their dependents.

The arrangement is altogether a most improvident one for society, whose interest it is to produce the greatest amount of wealth of the best qualities; while the existing system of distribution is not only to withdraw great numbers from producing to become distributors, but to add to the cost of the consumer all the expense of a most wasteful and extravagant distribution; the distribution costing to the consumer many times the price of the original cost of the wealth purchased.

Then, by the position in which the seller is placed by his created desire for gain on the one hand, and the competition he meets with from opponents selling similar productions on the other, he is strongly tempted to deteriorate the articles which he has for sale; and when these are provisions, either of home production or of foreign importation, the effects upon the health, and consequent comfort and happiness of the consumers, are often most injurious, and productive of much premature death, especially among the working classes, who, in this respect, are perhaps made to be the greatest sufferers, by purchasing the inferior or low-priced articles. . . .

The expense of thus distributing wealth in Great Britain and Ireland, including transit from place to place, and all the agents directly and indirectly engaged in this department is, perhaps, little short of one hundred millions annually, without taking into consideration the deterioration of the quality of many of the articles constituting this wealth, by carriage, and by being divided into small quantities, and kept in improper stores and places, in which the atmosphere is unfavorable to the keeping of such articles in a tolerably good, and much less in the best, condition for use.

In further illustration of the contrariety of interests between person and person, class and class, which pervades the present constitution of society, M. Considérant adds:

If the wine-growers wish for free trade, this freedom ruins the producer of corn, the manufacturers of iron, of cloth, of cotton, and—we are compelled to add—the smuggler and the customs' officer. If it is the interest of the consumer that machines should be invented which lower prices by rendering production less costly, these same machines throw out of work thousands of workmen who do not know how to, and cannot at once, find other work. Here, then, again is one of the innumerable *vicious circles* of civilization . . . for there are a thousand facts which prove cumulatively that in our existing social system the introduction of any good brings always along with it some evil.

In short, if we go lower down and come to vulgar details, we find that it is the interest of the tailor, the shoemaker, and the hatter that coats, shoes, and hats should be soon worn out; that the glazier profits by the hail-storms which break windows; that the mason and the architect profit by fires; the lawyer is enriched by lawsuits; the doctor by disease; the wine-seller by drunkenness; the prostitute by debauchery. And what a disaster would it be for the judges, the police, and the gaolers, as well as for the barristers and the solicitors, and all the lawyers' clerks if crimes, offenses, and lawsuits were all at once to come to an end![6]

The following is one of the cardinal points of this school:

Add to all this, that civilization, which sows dissension and war on every side; which employs a great part of its powers in unproductive labor, or even in destruction; which furthermore diminishes the public wealth by the unnecessary friction and discord it introduces into industry; add to all this, I say, that this same social system has for its special characteristic to produce a repugnance for work—a disgust for labor.

Everywhere you hear the laborer, the artisan, the clerk complain of his position and his occupation, while they long for the time when they can retire from work imposed upon them by necessity. To be repugnant, to have for its motive and pivot nothing but the fear of starvation, is the great, the fatal, characteristic of civilized labor. The civilized workman is condemned to penal servitude. So long as productive labor is so organized that instead of being associated with pleasure it is associated with pain, weariness and dislike, it will always happen that all will avoid it who are able. With few exceptions, those only will consent to work who are compelled to it by want. Hence the most numerous classes, the artificers of social wealth, the active and direct creators of all comfort and luxury, will always be condemned to touch closely on poverty and hunger; they will always be the slaves to ignorance and degradation; they will continue to be always that huge herd of mere beasts of burden whom we see ill-grown, decimated by disease, bowed down in the great workshop of society over the plough or over the counter, that they may prepare the delicate food, and the sumptuous enjoyments of the upper and idle classes.

So long as no method of attractive labor has been devised, it will continue to be true that "there must be many poor in order that there may be a few rich"; a mean and hateful saying, which we hear every day quoted as an eternal truth from the mouths of people who call themselves Christians or philosophers! It is very easy to understand that oppression, trickery, and especially poverty, are the permanent and fatal appanage of every state of society characterized by the dislike of work, for, in this case, there is nothing but poverty that will force men to labor. And the proof of this is, that if every one of all the workers were to become suddenly rich, nineteen-twentieths of all the work now done would be abandoned.[7]

In the opinion of the Fourierists, the tendency of the present order of society is to a concentration of wealth in the hands of a comparatively few immensely rich individuals or companies, and the reduction of all the rest of the community into a complete dependence on them. This was termed by Fourier *la féodalité industrielle*.

"This feudalism," says M. Considérant, "would be constituted as soon as the largest part of the industrial and territorial property of the nation belongs to a minority which absorbs all its revenues, while the great majority, chained to the work-bench or laboring on the soil, must be content to gnaw the pittance which is cast to them."[8]

This disastrous result is to be brought about partly by the mere progress of competition, as sketched in our previous extract by M. Louis Blanc; assisted by the progress of national debts, which M. Considérant regards as mortgages of the whole land and capital of the country, of which "les capitalistes prêteurs" become, in a greater and greater measure, co-proprietors, receiving without labor or risk an increasing portion of the revenues.

NOTES

1. See Louis Blanc, "Organisation du Travail," 4me édition, pp. 6, 11, 53, 57.
2. See Louis Blanc, "Organisation du Travail," pp. 58-61, 65-66, 4me édition. Paris, 1845.
3. See Considérant, "Destinée Sociale," tome i. pp. 35, 36, 37, 3me éd. Paris, 1848.
4. See "Destinée Sociale," par V. Considérant, tome i. pp. 38-40.
5. See Considérant, "Destinée Sociale," tome i. pp. 43-51, 3me édition, Paris, 1848.
6. Considérant, "Destinée Sociale," tome i., pp. 59, 60.
7. Considérant, "Destinée Sociale," tome i., pp. 60, 61.
8. "Destinée Sociale," tome i., p. 134.

Three

The Socialist Objections to the
Present Order of Society Examined

It is impossible to deny that the considerations brought to notice in the preceding chapter make out a frightful case either against the existing order of society, or against the position of man himself in this world. How much of the evils should be referred to the one, and how much to the other, is the principal theoretic question which has to be resolved. But the strongest case is susceptible of exaggeration; and it will have been evident to many readers, even from the passages I have quoted, that such exaggeration is not wanting in the representations of the ablest and most candid Socialists. Though much of their allegations is un-

97

answerable, not a little is the result of errors in political economy; by which, let me say once for all, I do not mean the rejection of any practical rules of policy which have been laid down by political economists, I mean ignorance of economic facts, and of the causes by which the economic phenomena of society as it is, are actually determined.

In the first place, it is unhappily true that the wages of ordinary labor, in all the countries of Europe, are wretchedly insufficient to supply the physical and moral necessities of the population in any tolerable measure. But, when it is further alleged that even this insufficient remuneration has a tendency to diminish; that there is, in the words of M. Louis Blanc, *une baisse continue des salaires;* the assertion is in opposition to all accurate information, and to many notorious facts. It has yet to be proved that there is any country in the civilized world where the ordinary wages of labor, estimated either in money or in articles of consumption, are declining; while in many they are, on the whole, on the increase; and an increase which is becoming, not slower, but more rapid. There are, occasionally, branches of industry which are being gradually superseded by something else, and, in those, until production accommodates itself to demand, wages are depressed; which is an evil, but a temporary one, and would admit of great alleviation even in the present system of social economy. A diminution thus produced of the reward of labor in some particular employment is the effect and the evidence of increased remuneration, or of a new source of remuneration, in some other; the total and the average remuneration being undiminished, or even increased. To make out an appearance of diminution in the rate of wages in any leading branch of industry, it is always found necessary to compare some month or year of special and temporary depression at the present time, with the average rate, or even some exceptionally high rate, at an earlier time. The vicissitudes are no doubt a great evil, but they were as frequent and as severe in former periods of economical history as now. The greater scale of the transactions, and the greater number of persons involved in each fluctuation, may make the fluctuation appear greater, but though a larger population affords more sufferers, the evil does not weigh heavier on each of them individually. There is much evidence of improvement, and none, that is at all trustworthy, of deterioration, in the mode of living of the laboring population of the countries of Europe; when there is any appearance to the contrary it is local or partial, and can always be traced either to the pressure of some temporary calamity, or to some bad law or unwise act of government which admits of being corrected, while the permanent causes all operate in the direction of improvement.

M. Louis Blanc, therefore, while showing himself much more enlightened than the older school of levellers and democrats, inasmuch as he recognizes the connection between low wages and the over-rapid increase of population, appears to have fallen into the same error which was at first committed by Malthus and his followers, that of supposing that because population has a greater power of increase than subsistence, its pressure upon subsistence must be always growing more severe. The difference is that the early Malthusians thought this an irrepressible tendency, while M. Louis Blanc thinks that it can be repressed, but only under a system of Communism. It is a great point gained for truth when it comes to be seen that the tendency to over-popula-

tion is a fact which Communism, as well as the existing
order of society, would have to deal with. And it is much to
be rejoiced at that this necessity is admitted by the most
considerable chiefs of all existing schools of Socialism. Owen
and Fourier, no less than M. Louis Blanc, admitted it, and
claimed for their respective systems a preeminent power of
dealing with this difficulty. However this may be, experience
shows that in the existing state of society the pressure of
population on subsistence, which is the principal cause of
low wages, though a great, is not an increasing evil; on the
contrary, the progress of all that is called civilization has a
tendency to diminish it, partly by the more rapid increase of
the means of employing and maintaining labor, partly by the
increased facilities opened to labor for transporting itself to
new countries and unoccupied fields of employment, and
partly by a general improvement in the intelligence and prudence of the population. This progress, no doubt, is slow;
but it is much that such progress should take place at all,
while we are still only in the first stage of that public movement for the education of the whole people, which when
more advanced must add greatly to the force of all the two
causes of improvement specified above. It is, of course, open
to discussion what form of society has the greatest power of
dealing successfully with the pressure of population on subsistence, and on this question there is much to be said for
Socialism; what was long thought to be its weakest point
will, perhaps, prove to be one of its strongest. But it has no
just claim to be considered as the sole means of preventing
the general and growing degradation of the mass of mankind
through the peculiar tendency of poverty to produce over-
population. Society as at present constituted is not descend-

ing into that abyss, but gradually, though slowly, rising out of it, and this improvement is likely to be progressive if bad laws do not interfere with it.

Next, it must be observed that Socialists generally, and even the most enlightened of them, have a very imperfect and one-sided notion of the operation of competition. They see half its effects, and overlook the other half; they regard it as an agency for grinding down everyone's remuneration—for obliging everyone to accept less wages for his labor, or a less price for his commodities, which would be true only if everyone had to dispose of his labor or his commodities to some great monopolist, and the competition were all on one side. They forget that competition is a cause of high prices and values as well as of low; that the buyers of labor and of commodities compete with one another as well as the sellers; and that if it is competition which keeps the prices of labor and commodities as low as they are, it is competition which prevents them from falling still lower. In truth, when competition is perfectly free on both sides, its tendency is not specially either to raise or to lower the price of articles, but to equalize it; to level inequalities of remuneration, and to reduce all to a general average, a result which, in so far as realized (no doubt very imperfectly), is, on Socialistic principles, desirable. But if, disregarding for the time that part of the effects of competition which consists in keeping up prices, we fix our attention on its effect in keeping them down, and contemplate this effect in reference solely to the interest of the laboring classes, it would seem that if competition keeps down wages, and so gives a motive to the laboring classes to withdraw the labor market from the full influence of competition, if they can, it must on the other hand have credit for keeping down the prices of the articles on which wages are expended, to the great advantage of those who depend on wages. To meet this consideration Socialists, as we said in our quotation from M. Louis Blanc, are reduced to affirm that the low prices of commodities produced by competition are delusive and lead in the end to higher prices than before, because when the richest competitor has got rid of all his rivals, he commands the market and can demand any price he pleases. Now, the commonest experience shows that this state of things, under really free competition, is wholly imaginary. The richest competitor neither does nor can get rid of all his rivals, and establish himself in exclusive possession of the market; and it is not the fact that any important branch of industry or commerce formerly divided among many has become, or shows any tendency to become, the monopoly of a few.

The kind of policy described is sometimes possible where, as in the case of railways, the only competition possible is between two or three great companies, the operations being on too vast a scale to be within the reach of individual capitalists; and this is one of the reasons why businesses which require to be carried on by great joint-stock enterprises cannot be trusted to competition, but, when not reserved by the State to itself, ought to be carried on under conditions prescribed, and, from time to time, varied by the State, for the purpose of insuring to the public a cheaper supply of its wants than would be afforded by private interest in the absence of sufficient competition. But in the ordinary branches of industry no one rich competitor has it in his power to drive out all the smaller ones. Some businesses show a tendency to pass out of the hands of many small producers or dealers into a smaller number of larger ones; but the cases in which this happens are those in which the possession of a larger capital permits the adoption of more powerful machinery, more efficient by more expensive processes, or a better organized and more economical mode of carrying on business, and thus enables the large dealer legitimately and permanently to supply the commodity cheaper than can be done on the small scale; to the great advantage of the consumers, and therefore of the laboring classes, and diminishing, *pro tanto,* that waste of the resources of the community so much complained of by Socialists, the unnecessary multiplication of mere distributors, and of the various other classes whom Fourier calls the parasites of industry. When this change is effected, the larger capitalists, either individual or joint-stock, among which the business is divided, are seldom, if ever, in any considerable branch of commerce, so few as that competition shall not continue to act between them; so that the saving in cost, which enabled them to undersell the small dealers, continues afterwards, as at first, to be passed on, in lower prices, to their customers. The operation, therefore, of competition in keeping down the prices of commodities, including those on which wages are expended, is not illusive, but real, and, we may add, is a growing, not a declining, fact.

But there are other respects, equally important, in which the charges brought by Socialists against competition do not admit of so complete an answer. Competition is the best security for cheapness, but by no means a security for quality. In former times, when producers and consumers were less numerous, it was a security for both. The market was not large enough nor the means of publicity sufficient to enable a dealer to make a fortune by continually attracting new customers: his success depended on his retaining those that he had; and when a dealer furnished good articles, or when he did not, the fact was soon known to those whom it concerned, and he acquired a character for honest or dishonest dealing of more importance to him than the gain that would be made by cheating casual purchasers. But on the great scale of modern transactions, with the great multiplication of competition and the immense increase in the quantity of business competed for, dealers are so little dependent on permanent customers that character is much less essential to them, while there is also far less certainty of their obtaining the character they deserve. The low prices which a tradesman advertises are known, to a thousand for one who has discovered for himself or learned from others, that the bad quality of the goods is more than an equivalent for their cheapness; while at the same time the much greater fortunes now made by some dealers excite the cupidity of all, and the greed of rapid gain substitutes itself for the modest desire to make a living by their business. In this manner, as wealth increases and greater prizes seem to be within reach, more and more of a gambling spirit is introduced into commerce; and where this prevails not only are the simplest maxims of prudence disregarded, but all, even the most perilous, forms of pecuniary improbity receive a terrible stimulus. This is the meaning of what is called the intensity of modern competition. It is further to be mentioned that when this intensity has reached a certain height, and when a portion of the producers of an article or the dealers in it have resorted to any of the modes of fraud, such as adulteration, giving short measure, &c., of the increase of which there is now so much complaint, the temptation is immense on these to adopt the fraudulent practices, who would not have originated them; for the public are aware of the low prices fallaciously produced by the frauds, but do not find out at first, if ever, that the article is not worth the lower price, and they will not go on paying a higher price for a better article, and the honest dealer is placed at a terrible disadvantage. Thus the frauds, begun by a few, become customs of the trade, and the morality of the trading classes is more and more deteriorated.

On this point, therefore, Socialists have really made out the existence not only of a great evil, but of one which grows and tends to grow with the growth of population and wealth. It must be said, however, that society has never yet used the means which are already in its power of grappling with this evil. The laws against commercial frauds are very defective, and their execution still more so. Laws of this description have no chance of being really enforced unless it is the special duty of some one to enforce them. They are specially in need of a public prosecutor. It is still to be discovered how far it is possible to repress by means of the criminal law a class of misdeeds which are now seldom brought before the tribunals, and to which, when brought, the judicial administration of this country is most unduly lenient. The most important class, however, of these frauds, to the mass of the people, those which affect the price or quality of articles of daily consumption, can be in a great measure overcome by the institution of cooperative stores. By this plan any body of consumers who form themselves into an association for the purpose, are enabled to pass over the retail dealers and obtain their articles direct from the wholesale merchants, or, what is better (now that wholesale cooperative agencies have

been established), from the producers, thus freeing themselves from the heavy tax now paid to the distributing classes
and at the same time eliminate the usual perpetrators of
adulterations and other frauds. Distribution thus becomes a
work performed by agents selected and paid by those who
have no interest in anything but the cheapness and goodness
of the article; and the distributors are capable of being 'hus
reduced to the numbers which the quantity of work to be
done really requires. The difficulties of the plan consist in
the skill and trustworthiness required in the managers, and
the imperfect nature of the control which can be exercised
over them by the body at large. The great success and rapid
growth of the system prove, however, that these difficulties
are, in some tolerable degree, overcome. At all events, if the
beneficial tendency of the competition of retailers in promoting cheapness is foregone, and has to be replaced by other
securities, the mischievous tendency of the same competition
in deteriorating quality is at any rate got rid of; and the
prosperity of the cooperative stores shows that this benefit is
obtained not only without detriment to cheapness, but with
great advantage to it, since the profits of the concerns enable
them to return to the consumers a large percentage on the
price of every article supplied to them. So far, therefore, as
this class of evils is concerned, an effectual remedy is already in operation, which, though suggested by and partly
grounded on socialistic principles, is consistent with the existing constitution of property.

   With regard to those greater and more conspicuous
economical frauds, or malpractices equivalent to frauds, of
which so many deplorable cases have become notorious—
committed by merchants and bankers between themselves or

between them and those who have trusted them with money, such a remedy as above described is not available, and the only resources which the present constitution of society affords against them are a sterner reprobation by opinion, and a more efficient repression by the law. Neither of these remedies has had any approach to an effectual trial. It is on the occurrence of insolvencies that these dishonest practices usually come to light; the perpetrators take their place, not in the class of malefactors, but in that of insolvent debtors; and the laws of this and other countries were formerly so savage against simple insolvency, that by one of those reactions to which the opinions of mankind are liable, insolvents came to be regarded mainly as objects of compassion, and it seemed to be thought that the hand both of law and of public opinion could hardly press too lightly upon them. By an error in a contrary direction to the ordinary one of our law, which in the punishment of offenses in general wholly neglects the question of reparation to the sufferer, our bankruptcy laws have for some time treated the recovery for creditors of what is left of their property as almost the sole object, scarcely any importance being attached to the punishment of the bankrupt for any misconduct which does not directly interfere with that primary purpose. For three or four years past there has been a slight counter-reaction, and more than one bankruptcy act has been passed, somewhat less indulgent to the bankrupt; but the primary object regarded has still been the pecuniary interest of the creditors, and criminality in the bankrupt himself, with the exception of a small number of well-marked offenses, gets off almost with impunity. It may be confidently affirmed, therefore, that, at least in this country, society has not exerted the

power it possesses of making mercantile dishonesty danger-
ous to the perpetrator. On the contrary, it is a gambling trick
in which all the advantage is on the side of the trickster: if the
trick succeeds it makes his fortune, or preserves it; if it fails,
he is at most reduced to poverty, which was perhaps already
impending when he determined to run the chance, and he is
classed by those who have not looked closely into the matter,
and even by many who have, not among the infamous but
among the unfortunate. Until a more moral and rational
mode of dealing with culpable insolvency has been tried and
failed, commercial dishonesty cannot be ranked among evils
the prevalence of which is inseparable from commercial
competition.

Another point on which there is much misapprehension
on the part of Socialists, as well as of Trades Unionists and
other partisans of Labor against Capital, relates to the proportions in which the produce of the country is really shared
and the amount of what is actually diverted from those who
produce it, to enrich other persons. I forbear for the present
to speak of the land, which is a subject apart. But with
respect to capital employed in business, there is in the popular notions a great deal of illusion. When, for instance, a
capitalist invests £20,000 in his business, and he draws from
it an income of (suppose) £2,000 a year, the common impression is as if he was the beneficial owner both of the
£20,000 and of the £2,000, while the laborers own nothing
but their wages. The truth, however, is that he only obtains
the £2,000 on condition of applying no part of the £20,000
to his own use. He has the legal control over it, and might
squander it if he chose, but if he did he would not have the
£2,000 a year also. As long as he derives an income from his

capital he has not the option of withholding it from the use of others. As much of his invested capital as consists of buildings, machinery, and other instruments of production, are applied to production and are not applicable to the support or enjoyment of any one. What is so applicable (including what is laid out in keeping up or renewing the buildings and instruments) is paid away to laborers, forming their remuneration and their share in the division of the produce. For all personal purposes they have the capital and he has but the profits, which it only yields to him on condition that the capital itself is employed in satisfying not his own wants, but those of laborers. The proportion which the profits of capital usually bear to the capital itself (or rather to the circulating portion of it) is the ratio which the capitalist's share of the produce bears to the aggregate share of the laborers. Even of his own share a small part only belongs to him as the owner of capital. The portion of the produce which falls to capital merely as capital is measured by the interest of money, since that is all that the owner of capital obtains when he contributes nothing to production except the capital itself. Now the interest of capital in the public funds, which are considered to be the best security, is at the present prices (which have not varied much for many years) about three and one-third percent. Even in this investment there is some little risk—risk of repudiation, risk of being obliged to sell out at a low price in some commercial crisis.

Estimating these risks at 1/3 percent, the remaining 3 percent may be considered as the remuneration of capital, apart from insurance against loss. On the security of a mortgage 4 percent is generally obtained, but in this transaction there are considerably greater risks—the uncertainty of titles to land under our bad system of law; the chance of having to realize the security at a great cost in law charges; and liability to delay in the receipt of the interest, even when the principal is safe. When mere money independently of exertion yields a larger income, as it sometimes does, for example, by shares in railway or other companies, the surplus is hardly ever an equivalent for the risk of losing the whole, or part, of the capital by mismanagement, as in the case of the Brighton Railway, the dividend of which, after having been 6 percent per annum, sunk to from nothing to 1½ percent, and shares which had been bought at 120 could not be sold for more than about 43. When money is lent at the high rates of interest one occasionally hears of, rates only given by spendthrifts and needy persons, it is because the risk of loss is so great that few who possess money can be induced to lend to them at all. So little reason is there for the outcry against "usury" as one of the grievous burthens of the working classes. Of the profits, therefore, which a manufacturer or other person in business obtains from his capital no more than about 3 percent can be set down to the capital itself. If he were able and willing to give up the whole of this to his laborers, who already share among them the whole of his capital as it is annually reproduced from year to year, the addition of their weekly wages would be inconsiderable. Of what he obtains beyond 3 percent a great part is insurance against the manifold losses he is exposed to, and cannot safely be applied to his own use, but requires to be kept in reserve to cover those losses when they occur. The remainder is properly the remuneration of his skill and industry—the wages of his labor of superintendence. No doubt if he is very successful in business these wages of his are extremely liberal, and quite out of proportion to what the same skill and industry would command if offered for hire. But, on the other hand, he runs a worse risk than that of being out of employment; that of doing the work without earning anything by it, of having the labor and anxiety without the wages. I do not say that the drawbacks balance the privileges, or that he derives no advantage from the position which makes him a capitalist and employer of labor, instead of a skilled superintendent letting out his services to others; but the amount of his advantage must not be estimated by the great prizes alone. If we subtract from the gains of some the losses of others, and deduct from the balance a fair compensation for the anxiety, skill, and labor of both, grounded on the market price of skilled superintendence, what remains will be, no doubt, considerable, but yet, when compared to the entire capital of the country, annually reproduced and dispensed in wages, it is very much smaller than it appears to the popular imagination; and were the whole of it added to the share of the laborers it would make a less addition to that share than would be made by any important invention in machinery, or by the suppression of unnecessary distributors and other "parasites of industry." To complete the estimate, however, of the portion of the produce of industry which goes to remunerate capital we must not stop at the interest earned out of the produce by the capital actually employed in producing it, but must include that which is paid to the former owners of capital which has been unproductively spent and no longer exists, and is paid, of course, out of the produce of other capital. Of this nature is the interest of national debts, which is the cost a nation is burthened with for past difficulties and dangers, or for past folly or profligacy of its rulers, more or less shared by the nation itself. To this must be added the interest on the debts of landowners and other unproductive consumers; except so far as the money borrowed may have been spent in remunerative improvement of the productive powers of the land. As for landed property itself—the appropriation of the rent of land by private individuals—I reserve, as I have said, this question for discussion hereafter; for the tenure of land might be varied in any manner considered desirable, all the land might be declared the property of the State, without interfering with the right of property in anything which is the product of human labor and abstinence.

It seemed desirable to begin the discussion of the Socialist question by these remarks in abatement of Socialist exaggerations, in order that the true issues between Socialism and the existing state of society might be correctly conceived. The present system is not, as many Socialists believe, hurrying us into a state of general indigence and slavery from which only Socialism can save us. The evils and injustices suffered under the present system are great, but they are not increasing; on the contrary, the general tendency is towards their slow diminution. Moreover the inequalities in the distribution of the produce between capital and labor, however they may shock the feeling of natural justice, would not by their mere equalization afford by any means so large a fund for raising the lower levels of remuneration as Socialists, and many besides Socialists, are apt to suppose. There is not any one abuse or injustice now prevailing in society by merely abolishing which the human race would pass out of suffering into happiness. What is incumbent on us is a calm comparison between two different systems of society, with a view of determining which of them affords the greatest resources for overcoming the inevitable difficulties of life. And if we find the answer to this question more difficult, and more dependent upon intellectual and moral conditions, than is usually thought, it is satisfactory to reflect that there is time before us for the question to work itself out on an experimental scale, by actual trial. I believe we shall find that no other test is possible of the practicability or beneficial operation of Socialist arrangements; but that the intellectual and moral grounds of Socialism deserve the most attentive study, as affording in many cases the guiding principles of the improvements necessary to give the present economic system of society its best chance.

Four

The Difficulties of Socialism

Among those who call themselves Socialists, two kinds of persons may be distinguished. There are, in the first place, those whose plans for a new order of society, in which private property and individual competition are to be superseded and other motives to action substituted, are on the scale of a village community or township, and would be applied to an entire country by the multiplication of such self-acting units; of this character are the systems of Owen, of Fourier, and the more thoughtful and philosophic Socialists generally. The other class, who are more a product of the Continent than of Great Britain and may be called the revolutionary Socialists, propose to themselves a much

bolder stroke. Their scheme is the management of the whole
productive resources of the country by one central authority,
the general government. And with this view some of them
avow as their purpose that the working classes, or somebody
in their behalf, should take possession of all the property of
the country, and administer it for the general benefit.

Whatever be the difficulties of the first of these two
forms of Socialism, the second must evidently involve the
same difficulties and many more. The former, too, has the
great advantage that it can be brought into operation progressively, and can prove its capabilities by trial. It can be
tried first on a select population and extended to others as
their education and cultivation permit. It need not, and in
the natural order of things would not, become an engine of
subversion until it had shown itself capable of being also a
means of reconstruction. It is not so with the other; the aim
of that is to substitute the new rule for the old at a single
stroke, and to exchange the amount of good realized under
the present system, and its large possibilities of improvement,
for a plunge without any preparation into the most extreme
form of the problem of carrying on the whole round of the
operations of social life without the motive power which has
always hitherto worked the social machinery. It must be
acknowledged that those who would play this game on the
strength of their own private opinion, unconfirmed as yet by
any experimental verification—who would forcibly deprive
all who have now a comfortable physical existence of their
only present means of preserving it, and would brave the
frightful bloodshed and misery that would ensue if the attempt was resisted—must have a serene confidence in their
own wisdom on the one hand and a recklessness of other

117

people's sufferings on the other, which Robespierre and St. Just, hitherto the typical instances of those united attributes, scarcely came up to. Nevertheless this scheme has great elements of popularity which the more cautious and reasonable form of Socialism has not; because what it professes to do it promises to do quickly, and holds out hope to the enthusiastic of seeing the whole of their aspirations realized in their own time and at a blow.

The peculiarities, however, of the revolutionary form of Socialism will be most conveniently examined after the considerations common to both the forms have been duly weighed.

The produce of the world could not attain anything approaching to its present amount, nor support anything approaching to the present number of its inhabitants, except upon two conditions: abundant and costly machinery, buildings, and other instruments of production; and the power of undertaking long operations and waiting a considerable time for their fruits. In other words, there must be a large accumulation of capital, both fixed in the implements and buildings, and circulating, that is, employed in maintaining the laborers and their families during the time which elapses before the productive operations are completed and the products come in. This necessity depends on physical laws, and is inherent in the condition of human life; but these requisites of production, the capital, fixed and circulating, of the country (to which has to be added the land, and all that is contained in it), may either be the collective property of those who use it, or may belong to individuals; and the question is, which of these arrangements is most conducive to human happiness. What is characteristic of Socialism is the joint ownership by all the members of the community of the instruments and means of production; which carries with it the consequence that the division of the produce among the body of owners must be a public act, performed according to rules laid down by the community. Socialism by no means excludes private ownership of articles of consumption; the exclusive right of each to his or her share of the produce when received, either to enjoy, to give, or to exchange it. The land, for example, might be wholly the property of the community for agricultural and other productive purposes, and might be cultivated on their joint account, and yet the dwelling assigned to each individual or family as part of their remuneration might be as exclusively theirs, while they continued to fulfill their share of the common labors, as any one's house now is; and not the dwelling only, but any ornamental ground which the circumstances of the association allowed to be attached to the house for purposes of enjoyment. The distinctive feature of Socialism is not that all things are in common, but that production is only carried on upon the common account, and that the instruments of production are held as common property. The *practicability* then of Socialism, on the scale of Mr. Owen's or M. Fourier's villages, admits of no dispute. The attempt to manage the whole production of a nation by one central organization is a totally different matter; but a mixed agricultural and manufacturing association of from two thousand to four thousand inhabitants under any tolerable circumstances of soil and climate would be easier to manage than many a joint stock company. The question to be considered is, whether this joint management is likely to be as efficient and successful as the managements of private industry by private capital. And this question has to be considered in a double aspect; the efficiency of the directing mind, or minds, and that of the simple workpeople. And in order to state this question in its simplest form, we will suppose the form of Socialism to be simple Communism, *i.e.,* equal division of the produce among all the sharers, or, according to M. Louis Blanc's still higher standard of justice, apportionment of it according to difference of need, but without making any difference of reward according to the nature of the duty nor according to the supposed merits or services of the individual. There are other forms of Socialism, particularly Fourierism, which do, on considerations of justice or expediency, allow differences of remuneration for different kinds or degrees of service to the community; but the consideration of these may be for the present postponed.

The difference between the motive powers in the economy of society under private property and under Communism would be greatest in the case of the directing minds. Under the present system, the direction being entirely in the hands of the person or persons who own (or are personally responsible for) the capital, the whole benefit of the difference between the best administration and the worst under which the business can continue to be carried on accrues to the person or persons who control the administration: they reap the whole profit of good management except so far as their self-interest or liberality induce them to share it with their subordinates; and they suffer the whole detriment of mismanagement except so far as this may cripple their subsequent power of employing labor. This strong personal motive to do their very best and utmost for the efficiency and economy of the operations, would not exist under Communism; as the managers would only receive out of the produce the same equal dividend as the other members of the association. What would remain would be the interest common to all in so managing affairs as to make the dividend as large as possible; the incentives of public spirit, of conscience, and of the honor and credit of the managers. The force of these motives, especially when combined, is great. But it varies greatly in different persons, and is much greater for some purposes than for others. The verdict of experience, in the imperfect degree of moral cultivation which mankind have yet reached, is that the motive of conscience and that of credit and reputation, even when they are of some strength, are, in the majority of cases, much stronger as restraining than as impelling forces—are more to be depended on for preventing wrong, than for calling forth the fullest energies in the pursuit of ordinary occupations. In the case of most men the only inducement which has been found sufficiently constant and unflagging to overcome the ever-present influence of indolence and love of ease, and induce men to apply themselves unrelaxingly to work for the most part in itself dull and unexciting, is the prospect of bettering their own economic condition and that of their family; and the closer the connection of every increase of exertion with a corresponding increase of its fruits, the more powerful is its motive. To suppose the contrary would be to imply that with men as they now are, duty and honor are more powerful principles of action than personal interest, not solely as to special acts and forbearances respecting which those sentiments have been exceptionally cultivated, but in the regulation of their whole lives; which no one, I suppose, will affirm. It may be said that this inferior efficacy of public and social feelings is not inevitable—is the result of imperfect education. This I am quite ready to admit, and also that there are even now many individual exceptions to the general infirmity. But before these exceptions can grow into a majority, or even into a very large minority, much time will be required. The education of human beings is one of the most difficult of all arts, and this is one of the points in which it has hitherto been least successful; moreover improvements in general education are necessarily very gradual, because the future generation is educated by the present, and the imperfections of the teachers set an invincible limit to the degree in which they can train their pupils to be better than themselves. We must therefore expect, unless we are operating upon a select portion of the population, that personal interest will for a long time be a more effective stimulus to the most vigorous and careful conduct of the industrial business of society than motives of a higher character. It will be said that at present the greed of personal gain by its very excess counteracts its own end by the stimulus it gives to reckless and often dishonest risks. This it does, and under Communism that source of evil would generally be absent. It is probable, indeed, that enterprise either of a bad or of a good kind would be a deficient element, and that business in general would fall very much under the dominion of routine; rather, as the performance of duty in such communities has to be enforced by external sanctions, the more nearly each person's duty can be reduced to fixed rules, the easier it is to hold him to its performance. A circumstance which increases the probability of this result is the limited power which the managers would have of independent action. They would of course hold their authority from the choice of the community, by whom their function might at any time be withdrawn from them; and this would make it necessary for them, even if not so required by the constitution of the community, to obtain the general consent of the body before making any change in the established mode of carrying on the concern. The difficulty of persuading a numerous body to make a change in their accustomed mode of working, of which change the trouble is often great, and the risk more obvious to their minds than the advantage, would have a great tendency to keep things in their accustomed track. Against this it has to be set, that choice by the persons who are directly interested in the success of the work, and who have practical knowledge and opportunities of judgment, might be expected on the average to produce managers of greater skill than the chances of birth, which now so often determine who shall be the owner of the capital. This may be true; and though it may be replied that the capitalist by inheritance can also, like the community, appoint a manager more capable than himself, this would only place him on the same level of advantage as the community, not on a higher level. But it must be said on the other side that under the Communist system the persons most qualified for the management would be likely very often to hang back from undertaking it. At present the manager, even if he be a hired servant, has a very much larger remuneration than the other persons concerned in the business; and there are open to his ambition higher social positions to which his function of manager is a stepping-stone. On the Communist system none of these advantages would be possessed by him; he could obtain only the same dividend out of the produce of the community's labor as any other member of it; he would no longer have the chance of raising himself from a receiver of wages into the class of capitalists; and while he could be in no way better off than any other laborer, his responsibilities and anxieties would be so much greater that a large proportion of mankind would be likely to prefer the less onerous position. This difficulty was foreseen by Plato as an objection to the system proposed in his Republic of community of goods among a governing class; and the motive on which he relied for inducing the fit persons to take on themselves, in the absence of all the ordinary inducements, the cares and labors of government, was the fear of being governed by worse men. This, in truth, is the motive which would have to be in the main depended upon; the persons most competent to the management would be prompted to undertake the office to prevent it from falling into less competent hands. And the motive would probably be effectual at times when there was an impression that by incompetent management the affairs of the community were going to ruin, or even only decidedly deteriorating. But this motive could not, as a rule, expect to be called into action by the less stringent inducement of merely promoting improvement; unless in the case of inventors or schemers eager to try some device from which they hoped for great and immediate fruits; and persons of this kind are very often unfitted by over-sanguine temper and imperfect judgment for the general conduct of affairs, while even when fitted for it they are precisely the kind of persons against whom the average man is apt to entertain a prejudice, and they would often be unable to overcome the preliminary difficulty of persuading the community both to adopt their project and to accept them as managers. Communistic management would thus be, in all probability, less favorable than private management to that striking out of new paths and making immediate sacrifices for distant and uncertain advantages, which, though seldom unattended with risk, is generally indispensable to great improvements in the economic condition of mankind, and even to keeping up the existing state in the face of a continual increase of the number of mouths to be fed.

We have thus far taken account only of the operation of motives upon the managing minds of the association. Let us now consider how the case stands in regard to the ordinary workers.

These, under Communism, would have no interest, except their share of the general interest, in doing their work honestly and energetically. But in this respect matters would be no worse than they now are in regard to the great majority of the producing classes. These, being paid by fixed wages, are so far from having any direct interest of their own in the efficiency of their work, that they have not even that share in the general interest which every worker would have in the Communistic organization. Accordingly, the inefficiency of hired labor, the imperfect manner in which it calls forth the real capabilities of the laborers, is matter of common remark. It is true that a character for being a good workman is far from being without its value, as it tends to give him a preference in employment, and sometimes obtains for him higher wages. There are also possibilities of rising to the position of foreman, or other subordinate administrative posts, which are not only more highly paid than ordinary labor, but sometimes open the way to ulterior advantages. But on the other side is to be set that under Communism the general sentiment of the community, composed of the comrades under whose eyes each person works, would be sure to be in favor of good and hard working, and unfavorable to laziness, carelessness, and waste. In the present system not only is this not the case, but the public opinion of the workman class often acts in the very opposite direction: the rules of some trade societies actually forbid their members to exceed a certain standard of efficiency, lest they should diminish the number of laborers required for the work; and for the same reason they often violently resist contrivances for economizing labor. The change from this to a state in which every person would have an interest in rendering every other person as industrious, skillful, and careful as possible (which would be the case under Communism), would be a change very much for the better.

It is, however, to be considered that the principal defects of the present system in respect to the efficiency of labor may be corrected, and the chief advantages of Communism in that respect may be obtained, by arrangements compatible with private property and individual competition. Considerable improvement is already obtained by piece-work, in the kinds of labor which admit of it. By this the workman's personal interest is closely connected with the quantity of work he turns out—not so much with its quality, the security for which still has to depend on the employer's vigilance; neither does piece-work carry with it the public opinion of the workman class, which is often, on the contrary, strongly opposed to it, as a means of (as they think) diminishing the market for laborers. And there is really good ground for their dislike of piece-work, if, as is alleged, it is a frequent practice of employers, after using piece-work to ascertain the utmost which a good workman can do, to fix the price of piece-work so low that by doing that utmost he is not able to earn more than they would be obliged to give him as day wages for ordinary work.

But there is a far more complete remedy than piece-work for the disadvantages of hired labor, viz. what is now called industrial partnership—the admission of the whole body of laborers to a participation in the profits, by distributing among all who share in the work, in the form of a percentage on their earnings, the whole or a fixed portion of the gains after a certain remuneration has been allowed to the capitalist. This plan has been found of admirable efficacy, both in this country and abroad. It has enlisted the sentiments of the workmen employed on the side of the most careful regard by all of them to the general interest of the concern; and by its joint effect in promoting zealous exertion and checking waste, it has very materially increased the remuneration of every description of labor in the concerns in which it has been adopted. It is evident that this system admits of indefinite extension and of an indefinite increase in the share of profits assigned to the laborers, short of that which would leave to the managers less than the needful degree of personal interest in the success of the concern. It is even likely that when such arrangements become common, many of these concerns would at some period or another, on the death or retirement of the chiefs, pass, by arrangement, into the state of purely cooperative associations.

It thus appears that as far as concerns the motives of exertion in the general body, Communism has no advantage which may not be reached under private property, while as respects the managing heads it is at a considerable disadvantage. It has also some disadvantages which seem to be inherent in it, through the necessity under which it lies of deciding in a more or less arbitrary manner questions which, on the present system, decide themselves, often badly enough, but spontaneously.

It is a simple rule, and under certain aspects a just one, to give equal payment to all who share in the work. But this is a very imperfect justice unless the work also is apportioned equally. Now the many different kinds of work required in every society are very unequal in hardness and unpleasantness. To measure these against one another, so as to make quality equivalent to quantity, is so difficult that Communists generally propose that all should work by turns at every kind of labor. But this involves an almost complete sacrifice of the economic advantages of the division of employments, advantages which are indeed frequently overestimated (or rather the counter-considerations are underestimated) by political economists, but which are nevertheless, in the point of view of the productiveness of labor, very considerable, for the double reason that the cooperation of employment enables the work to distribute itself with some regard to the special capacities and qualifications of the worker, and also that every worker acquires greater skill and rapidity in one kind of work by confining himself to it. The arrangement, therefore, which is deemed indispensable to a just distribution would probably be a very considerable disadvantage in respect of production. But further, it is still a very imperfect standard of justice to demand the same amount of work from every one. People have unequal capacities of work, both mental and bodily, and what is a light task for one is an insupportable burthen to another. It is necessary, therefore, that there should be a dispensing power, an authority competent to grant exemptions from the ordinary amount of work, and to proportion tasks in some measure to capabilities. As long as there are any lazy or selfish persons who like better to be worked for by others than to work, there will be frequent attempts to obtain exemptions by favor or fraud, and the frustration of these attempts will be an affair of considerable difficulty, and will by no means be always successful. These inconveniences would be little felt, for some time at least, in communities composed of select persons, earnestly desirous of the success of the experiment; but plans for the regeneration of society must consider average human beings, and not only them but the large residuum of persons greatly below the average in the personal and social virtues. The squabbles and ill-blood which could not fail to be engendered by the distribution of work whenever such persons have to be dealt with, would be a great abatement from the harmony and unanimity which Communists hope would be found among the members of their association. That concord would, even in the most fortunate circumstances, be much more liable to disturbance than Communists suppose. The institution provides that there shall be no quarrelling about material interests; individualism is excluded from that department of affairs. But there are other departments from which no institutions can exclude it: there will still be rivalry for reputation and for personal power. When selfish ambition is excluded from the field in which, with most men, it chiefly exercises itself, that of riches and pecuniary interest, it would betake itself with greater intensity to the domain still open to it, and we may expect that the struggles for preeminence and for influence in the management would be of great bitterness when the personal passions, diverted from their ordinary channel, are driven to seek their principal gratification in that other direction. For these various reasons it is probable that a Communist association would frequently fail to exhibit the attractive picture of mutual love and unity of will and feeling which we are often told by Communists to expect, but would often be torn by dissension and not unfrequently broken up by it.

Other and numerous sources of discord are inherent in the necessity which the Communist principle involves, of deciding by the general voice questions of the utmost importance to every one, which on the present system can be and are left to individuals to decide, each for his own case. As an example, take the subject of education. All Socialists are strongly impressed with the all-importance of the training given to the young, not only for the reasons which apply universally, but because their demands being much greater than those of any other system upon the intelligence and morality of the individual citizen, they have even more at stake than any other societies on the excellence of their educational arrangements. Now under Communism these arrangements would have to be made for every citizen by the collective body, since individual parents, supposing them to prefer some other mode of educating their children, would have no private means of paying for it, and would be limited to what they could do by their own personal teaching and influence. But every adult member of the body would have an equal voice in determining the collective system designed for the benefit of all. Here, then, is a most fruitful source of discord in every association. All who had any opinion or preference as to the education they would desire for their own children, would have to rely for their chance of obtaining it upon the influence they could exercise in the joint decision of the community.

It is needless to specify a number of other important questions affecting the mode of employing the productive resources of the association, the conditions of social life, the relations of the body with other associations, &c., on which difference of opinion, often irreconcilable, would be likely to arise. But even the dissensions which might be expected would be a far less evil to the prospects of humanity than a delusive unanimity produced by the prostration of all individual opinions and wishes before the decree of the majority. The obstacles to human progression are always great, and require a concurrence of favorable circumstances to overcome them; but an indispensable condition of their being overcome is, that human nature should have freedom to expand spontaneously in various directions, both in thought and practice; that people should both think for themselves and try experiments for themselves, and should not resign into the hands of rulers, whether acting in the name of a few or of the majority, the business of thinking for them, and of prescribing how they shall act. But in Communist associations private life would be brought in a most unexampled degree within the dominion of public authority, and there would be less scope for the development of individual character and individual preferences than has hitherto existed among the full citizens of any state belonging to the progressive branches of the human family. Already in all societies the compression of individuality by the majority is a great and growing evil; it would probably be much greater under Communism, except so far as it might be in the power of individuals to set bounds to it by selecting to belong to a community of persons like-minded with themselves.

From these various considerations I do not seek to draw any inference against the possibility that Communistic production is capable of being at some future time the form of society best adapted to the wants and circumstances of mankind. I think that this is, and will long be, an open question, upon which fresh light will continually be obtained, both by trial of the Communistic principle under favorable circumstances, and by the improvements which will be gradually effected in the working of the existing system, that of private ownership. The one certainty is, that Communism, to be successful, requires a high standard of both moral and intellectual education in all the members of the community— moral, to qualify them for doing their part honestly and energetically in the labor of life under no inducement but their share in the general interest of the association, and their feelings of duty and sympathy towards it; intellectual, to make them capable of estimating distant interests and entering into complex considerations, sufficiently at least to be able to discriminate, in these matters, good counsel from bad. Now I reject altogether the notion that it is impossible for education and cultivation such as is implied in these things to be made the inheritance of every person in the nation; but I am convinced that it is very difficult, and that the passage to it from our present condition can only be slow. I admit the plea that in the points of moral education on which the success of Communism depends, the present state of society is demoralizing, and that only a Communistic association can effectually train mankind for Communism. It is for Communism, then, to prove, by practical experiment, its power of giving this training. Experiments alone can show whether there is as yet in any portion of the population a sufficiently high level of moral cultivation to make Communism succeed, and to give to the next generation among themselves the education necessary to keep up that high level permanently. If Communist associations show that they can be durable and prosperous, they will multiply, and will probably be adopted by successive portions of the population of the more advanced countries as they become morally fitted for that mode of life. But to force unprepared populations into Communist societies, even if a political revolution gave the power to make such an attempt, would end in disappointment.

If practical trial is necessary to test the capabilities of Communism, it is no less required for those other forms of Socialism which recognize the difficulties of Communism and contrive means to surmount them. The principal of these is Fourierism, a system which, if only as a specimen of intellectual ingenuity, is highly worthy of the attention of any student, either of society or of the human mind. There is scarcely an objection or a difficulty which Fourier did not foresee, and against which he did not make provision beforehand by self-acting contrivances, grounded, however, upon a less high principle of distributive justice than that of Communism, since he admits inequalities of distribution and individual ownership of capital, but not the arbitrary disposal of it. The great problem which he grapples with is how to make labor attractive, since, if this could be done, the principal difficulty of Socialism would be overcome. He maintains that no kind of useful labor is necessarily or universally repugnant, unless either excessive in amount or devoid of the stimulus of companionship and emulation, or regarded by mankind with contempt. The workers in a Fourierist village are to class themselves spontaneously in groups, each group undertaking a different kind of work, and the same person may be a member not only of one group but of any number; a certain minimum having first been set apart for the subsistence of every member of the community, whether capable or not of labor, the society divides the remainder of the produce among the different groups, in such shares as it finds attract to each the amount of labor required, and no more; if there is too great a run upon particular groups it is a sign that those groups are over-remunerated relatively to others; if any are neglected their remuneration must be made higher. The share of produce assigned to each group is divided in fixed proportions among three elements— labor, capital, and talent; the part assigned to talent being rewarded by the suffrages of the group itself, and it is hoped that among the variety of human capacities all, or nearly all, will be qualified to excel in some group or other. The remuneration for capital is to be such as is found sufficient to induce savings from individual consumption, in order to increase the common stock to such point as is desired. The number and ingenuity of the contrivances for meeting minor difficulties, and getting rid of minor inconveniences, is very remarkable. By means of these various provisions it is the expectation of Fourierists that the personal inducements to exertion for the public interest, instead of being taken away, would be made much greater than at present, since every increase of the service rendered would be much more certain of leading to increase of reward than it is now, when accidents of position have so much influence. The efficiency of labor, they therefore expect, would be unexampled, while the saving of labor would be prodigious, by diverting to useful occupations that which is now wasted on things useless or hurtful, and by dispensing with the vast number of superfluous distributors, the buying and selling for the whole community being managed by a single agency. The free choice of individuals as to their manner of life would be no further interfered with than would be necessary for gaining the full advantages of cooperation in the industrial operations. Altogether, the picture of a Fourierist community is both attractive in itself and requires less from common humanity than any other known system of Socialism; and it is much to be desired that the scheme should have that fair trial which alone can test the workableness of any new scheme of social life.[1]

The result of our review of the various difficulties of Socialism has led us to the conclusion that the various schemes for managing the productive resources of the country by public instead of private agency have a case for a trial, and some of them may eventually establish their claims to preference over the existing order of things, but that they are at present workable only by the *élite* of mankind, and have yet to prove their power of training mankind at large to the state of improvement which they presuppose. Far more, of course, may this be said of the more ambitious plan which aims at taking possession of the whole land and capital of the country, and beginning at once to administer it on the public account. Apart from all consideration of injustice to the present possessors, the very idea of conducting the whole industry of a country by direction from a single center is so obviously chimerical, that nobody ventures to propose any mode in which it should be done; and it can hardly be doubted that if the revolutionary Socialists attained their immediate object, and actually had the whole property of the country at their disposal, they would find no other practicable mode of exercising their power over it than that of dividing it into portions, each to be made over to the administration of a small Socialist community. The problem of management, which we have seen to be so difficult even to a select population well prepared beforehand, would be thrown down to be solved as best it could by aggregations united only by locality, or taken indiscriminately from the population, including all the malefactors, all the idlest and most vicious, the most incapable of steady industry, forethought, or self-control, and a majority who, though not equally degraded, are yet, in the opinion of Socialists themselves, as far as regards the qualities essential for the success of Socialism, profoundly demoralized by the existing state of society. It is saying but little to say that the introduction of Socialism under such conditions could have no effect but disastrous failure, and its apostles could have only the consolation that the order of society as it now exists would have perished first, and all who benefit by it would be involved in the common ruin—a consolation which to some of them would probably be real, for if appearances can be trusted the animating principle of too many of the revolutionary Socialists is hate; a very excusable hatred of existing evils, which would vent itself by putting an end to the present system at all costs even to those who suffer by it, in the hope that out of chaos would arise a better Kosmos, and in the impatience of desperation respecting any more gradual improvement. They are unaware that chaos is the very most unfavorable position for setting out in the construction of a Kosmos, and that many ages of conflict, violence, and tyrannical oppression of the weak by the strong must intervene; they know not that they would plunge mankind into the state of nature so forcibly described by Hobbes *(Leviathan,* Part I. ch. xiii.), where every man is an enemy to every man:

> In such condition there is no place for industry, because the fruit thereof is uncertain, and consequently no culture of the earth, no navigation, no use of the commodities that may be imported by sea, no commodious building, no instruments of moving and removing such things as require such force, no knowledge of the face of the earth, no account of time, no arts, no letters, no society; and, which is worst of all, continual fear and danger of violent death; and the life of man solitary, poor, nasty, brutish, and short.

If the poorest and most wretched members of a so-called civilized society are in as bad a condition as every one would be in that worst form of barbarism produced by the dissolution of civilized life, it does not follow that the way to raise them would be to reduce all others to the same miserable state. On the contrary, it is by the aid of the first who have risen that so many others have escaped from the general lot, and it is only by better organization of the same process that it may be hoped in time to succeed in raising the remainder.

NOTE

1. The principles of Fourierism are clearly set forth and powerfully defended in the various writings of M. Victor Considérant, especially that entitled *La Destinée Sociale;* but the curious inquirer will do well to study them in the writings of Fourier himself; where he will find unmistakable proofs of genius, mixed, however, with the wildest and most unscientific fancies respecting the physical world, and much interesting but rash speculation on the past and future history of humanity. It is proper to add that on some important social questions, for instance on marriage, Fourier had peculiar opinions, which, however, as he himself declares, are quite independent of, and separable from, the principles of his industrial system.

Five

The Idea of Private Property
not Fixed but Variable

The preceding considerations appear sufficient to show that an entire renovation of the social fabric, such as is contemplated by Socialism, establishing the economic constitution of society upon an entirely new basis, other than that of private property and competition, however valuable as an ideal, and even as a prophecy of ultimate possibilities, is not available as a present resource, since it requires from those who are to carry on the new order of things qualities both moral and intellectual, which require to be tested in all, and to be created in most; and this cannot be done by an Act of

Parliament, but must be, on the most favorable supposition, a work of considerable time. For a long period to come the principle of individual property will be in possession of the field; and even if in any country a popular movement were to place Socialists at the head of a revolutionary government, in however many ways they might violate private property, the institution itself would survive, and would either be accepted by them or brought back by their expulsion, for the plain reason that people will not lose their hold of what is at present their sole reliance for subsistence and security until a substitute for it has been got into working order. Even those, if any, who had shared among themselves what was the property of others would desire to keep what they had acquired, and to give back to property in the new hands the sacredness which they had not recognized in the old.

But though, for these reasons, individual property has presumably a long term before it, if only of provisional existence, we are not, therefore, to conclude that it must exist during that whole term unmodified, or that all the rights now regarded as appertaining to property belong to it inherently, and must endure while it endures. On the contrary, it is both the duty and the interest of those who derive the most direct benefit from the laws of property to give impartial consideration to all proposals for rendering those laws in any way less onerous to the majority. This, which would in any case be an obligation of justice, is an injunction of prudence also, in order to place themselves in the right against the attempts which are sure to be frequent to bring the Socialist forms of society prematurely into operation.

One of the mistakes oftenest committed, and which are the sources of the greatest practical errors in human affairs, is that of supposing that the same name always stands for the same aggregation of ideas. No word has been the subject of more of this kind of misunderstanding than the word property. It denotes in every state of society the largest powers of exclusive control over things (and sometimes, unfortunately, over persons) which the law accords, or which custom, in that state of society, recognizes; but these powers of exclusive use and control are very various, and differ greatly in different countries and in different states of society.

For instance, in early states of society, the right of property did not include the right of bequest. The power of disposing of property by will was in most countries of Europe a rather late institution; and long after it was introduced it continued to be limited in favor of what were called natural heirs. Where bequest is not permitted, individual property is only a life interest. And in fact, as has been so well and fully set forth by Sir Henry Maine in his most instructive work on Ancient Law, the primitive idea of property was that it belonged to the family, not the individual. The head of the family had the management and was the person who really exercised the proprietary rights. As in other respects, so in this, he governed the family with nearly despotic power. But he was not free so to exercise his power as to defeat the co-proprietors of the other portions; he could not so dispose of the property as to deprive them of the joint enjoyment or of the succession. By the laws and customs of some nations the property could not be alienated without the consent of the male children; in other cases the child could by law demand a division of the property and the assignment to him of his share, as in the story of the Prodigal Son. If the association kept together after the death of the head, some other member of it, not always his son, but often the eldest of the family, the strongest, or the one selected by the rest, succeeded to the management and to the managing rights, all the others retaining theirs as before. If, on the other hand, the body broke up into separate families, each of these took away with it a part of the property. I say the property, not the inheritance, because the process was a mere continuance of existing rights, not a creation of new; the manager's share alone lapsed to the association.

Then, again, in regard to proprietary rights over immovables (the principal kind of property in a rude age) these rights were of very varying extent and duration. By the Jewish law property in immovables was only a temporary concession; on the Sabbatical year it returned to the common stock to be redistributed; though we may surmise that in the historical times of the Jewish state this rule may have been successfully evaded. In many countries of Asia, before European ideas intervened, nothing existed to which the expression property in land, as we understand the phrase, is strictly applicable. The ownership was broken up among several distinct parties, whose rights were determined rather by custom than by law. The government was part owner, having the right to a heavy rent. Ancient ideas and even ancient laws limited the government share to some particular fraction of the gross produce, but practically there was no fixed limit. The government might make over its share to an individual, who then became possessed of the right of collection and all the other rights of the state, but not those of any private person connected with the soil. These private rights were of various kinds. The actual cultivators, or such of them as had been long settled on the land, had a right to retain possession; it was held unlawful to evict them while they paid the rent—a rent not in general fixed by agreement, but by the custom of the neighborhood. Between the actual cultivators and the state, or the substitute to whom the state had transferred its rights, there were intermediate persons with rights of various extent. There were officers of government who collected the state's share of the produce, sometimes for large districts, who, though bound to pay over to government all they collected, after deducting a percentage, were often hereditary officers. There were also, in many cases, village communities, consisting of the reputed descendants of the first settlers of a village, who shared among themselves either the land or its produce according to rules established by custom, either cultivating it themselves or employing others to cultivate it for them, and whose rights in the land approached nearer to those of a landed proprietor, as understood in England, than those of any other party concerned. But the proprietary right of the village was not individual, but collective; inalienable (the rights of individual sharers could only be sold or mortgaged with the consent of the community) and governed by fixed rules. In medieval Europe almost all land was held from the sovereign on tenure of service, either military or agricultural; and in Great Britain even now, when the services as well as all the reserved rights of the sovereign have long since fallen into disuse or been commuted for taxation, the theory of the law does not acknowledge an absolute right of property in land in any individual; the fullest landed proprietor known to the law, the freeholder, is but a "tenant" of the Crown. In Russia, even when the cultivators of the soil were serfs of the landed proprietor, his proprietary right in the land was limited by rights of theirs belonging to them as a collective body managing its own affairs, and with which he could not interfere. And in most of the countries of continental Europe when serfage was abolished or went out of use, those who had cultivated the land as serfs remained in possession of rights as well as subject to obligations. The great land reforms of Stein and his successors in Prussia consisted in abolishing both the rights and the obligations, and dividing the land bodily between the proprietor and the peasant, instead of leaving each of them with a limited right over the whole. In other cases, as in Tuscany, the *metayer* farmer is virtually co-proprietor with the landlord, since custom, though not law, guarantees to him a permanent possession and half the gross produce, so long as he fulfills the customary conditions of his tenure.

Again, if rights of property over the same things are of different extent in different countries, so also are they exercised over different things. In all countries at a former time, and in some countries still, the right of property extended and extends to the ownership of human beings. There has often been property in public trusts, as in judicial offices, and a vast multitude of others in France before the Revolution; there are still a few patent offices in Great Britain, though I believe they will cease by operation of law on the death of the present holders; and we are only now abolishing property in army rank. Public bodies, constituted and endowed for public purposes, still claim the same inviolable right of property in their estates which individuals have in theirs, and though a sound political morality does not acknowledge this claim, the law supports it. We thus see that the right of property is differently interpreted, and held to be of different extent, in different times and places; that the conception entertained of it is a varying conception, has been frequently revised, and may admit of still further revision. It is also to be noticed that the revisions which it has hitherto undergone in the progress of society have generally been improvements. When, therefore, it is maintained, rightly or wrongly, that some change or modification in the powers exercised over things by the persons legally recognized as their proprietors would be beneficial to the public and conducive to the general improvement, it is no good answer to this merely to say that the proposed change conflicts with the idea of property. The idea of property is not some one thing, identical throughout history and incapable of alteration, but is variable like all other creations of the human mind; at any given time it is a brief expression denoting the rights over things conferred by the law or custom of some given society at that time; but neither on this point nor on any other has the law and custom of a given time and place a claim to be stereotyped for ever. A proposed reform in laws or customs is not necessarily objectionable because its adoption would imply, not the adaptation of all human affairs to the existing idea of property, but the adaptation of existing ideas of property to the growth and improvement of human affairs. This is said without prejudice to the equitable claim of proprietors to be compensated by the state for such legal rights of a proprietary nature as they may be dispossessed of for the public advantage. That equitable claim, the grounds and the just limits of it, are a subject by itself, and as such will be discussed hereafter. Under this condition, however, society is fully entitled to abrogate or alter any particular right of property which on sufficient consideration it judges to stand in the way of the public good. And assuredly the terrible case which, as we saw in a former chapter, Socialists are able to make out against the present economic order of society, demands a full consideration of all means by which the institution may have a chance of being made to work in a manner more beneficial to that large portion of society which at present enjoys the least share of its direct benefits.

THE SUBJECTION
OF WOMEN

THE SUBJECTION OF WOMEN

CHAPTER I

1. The object of this Essay is to explain, as clearly as I am able, the grounds of an opinion which I have held from the very earliest period when I had formed any opinions at all on social or political matters, and which, instead of being weakened or modified, has been constantly growing stronger by the progress of reflection and the experience of life: That the principle which regulates the existing social relations between the two sexes—the legal subordination of one sex to the other—is wrong in itself, and now one of the chief hindrances to human improvement; and that it ought to be replaced by a principle of perfect equality, admitting no power or privilege on the one side, nor disability on the other.

2. The very words necessary to express the task I have undertaken, show how arduous it is. But it would be a mistake to suppose that the difficulty of the case must lie in the insufficiency or obscurity of the grounds of reason on which my conviction rests. The difficulty is that which exists in all cases in which there is a mass of feeling to be contended against. So long as an opinion is strongly rooted in the feelings, it gains rather than loses in stability by having a preponderating weight of argument against it. For if it were accepted as a result of argument, the refutation of the argument might shake the solidity of the conviction; but when it rests solely on feeling, the worse it fares in argumentative contest, the more persuaded its adherents are that their feeling must have some deeper ground, which the arguments do not reach; and while the feeling remains, it is always throwing up fresh entrenchments of argument to repair any breach made in the old. And there are so many causes tending to make the feelings connected with this subject the most intense and most deeply-rooted of all those

which gather round and protect old institutions and customs,
that we need not wonder to find them as yet less undermined
and loosened than any of the rest by the progress of the great
modern spiritual and social transition; nor suppose that the barbarisms to which men cling longest must be less barbarisms than
those which they earlier shake off.

3. In every respect the burthen is hard on those who attack
an almost universal opinion. They must be very fortunate as
well as unusually capable if they obtain a hearing at all. They
have more difficulty in obtaining a trial, than any other litigants
have in getting a verdict. If they do extort a hearing, they
are subjected to a set of logical requirements totally different
from those exacted from other people. In all other cases, the
burthen of proof is supposed to lie with the affirmative. If a
person is charged with a murder, it rests with those who accuse
him to give proof of his guilt, not with himself to prove his
innocence. If there is a difference of opinion about the reality
of any alleged historical event, in which the feelings of men in
general are not much interested, as the Siege of Troy for
example, those who maintain that the event took place are
expected to produce their proofs, before those who take the
other side can be required to say anything; and at no time are
these required to do more than show that the evidence produced
by the others is of no value. Again, in practical matters, the
burthen of proof is supposed to be with those who are against
liberty; who contend for any restriction or prohibition; either
any limitation of the general freedom of human action, or any
disqualification or disparity of privilege affecting one person or
kind of persons, as compared with others. The *a priori* presumption is in favour of freedom and impartiality. It is held
that there should be no restraint not required by the general
good, and that the law should be no respecter of persons, but
should treat all alike, save where dissimilarity of treatment is
required by positive reasons, either of justice or of policy. But
of none of these rules of evidence will the benefit be allowed
to those who maintain the opinion I profess. It is useless for
me to say that those who maintain the doctrine that men have
a right to command and women are under an obligation to obey,
or that men are fit for government and women unfit, are on the
affirmative side of the question, and that they are bound to
show positive evidence for the assertions, or submit to their
rejection. It is equally unavailing for me to say that those who

deny to women any freedom or privilege rightly allowed to men, having the double presumption against them that they are opposing freedom and recommending partiality, must be held to the strictest proof of their case, and unless their success be such as to exclude all doubt, the judgment ought to go against them. These would be thought good pleas in any common case; but they will not be thought so in this instance. Before I could hope to make any impression, I should be expected not only to answer all that has ever been said by those who take the other side of the question, but to imagine all that could be said by them—to find them in reasons, as well as answer all I find: and besides refuting all arguments for the affirmative, I shall be called upon for invincible positive arguments to prove a negative. And even if I could do all this, and leave the opposite party with a host of unanswered arguments against them, and not a single unrefuted one on their side, I should be thought to have done little; for a cause supported on the one hand by universal usage, and on the other by so great a preponderance of popular sentiment, is supposed to have a presumption in its favour, superior to any conviction which an appeal to reason has power to produce in any intellects but those of a high class.

4. I do not mention these difficulties to complain of them; first, because it would be useless; they are inseparable from having to contend through people's understandings against the hostility of their feelings and practical tendencies: and truly the understandings of the majority of mankind would need to be much better cultivated than has ever yet been the case, before they can be asked to place such reliance in their own power of estimating arguments, as to give up practical principles in which they have been born and bred, and which are the basis of much of the existing order of the world, at the first argumentative attack which they are not capable of logically resisting. I do not therefore quarrel with them for having too little faith in argument, but for having too much faith in custom and the general feeling. It is one of the characteristic prejudices of the reaction of the nineteenth century against the eighteenth, to accord to the unreasoning elements in human nature the infallibility which the eighteenth century is supposed to have ascribed to the reasoning elements. For the apotheosis of Reason we have substituted that of Instinct; and we call everything instinct which we find in ourselves and for which we cannot trace any rational foundation. This idolatry, infinitely more degrading

than the other, and the most pernicious of the false worships of
the present day, of all of which it is now the main support, will
probably hold its ground until it gives way before a sound
psychology, laying bare the real root of much that is bowed
down to as the intention of Nature and the ordinance of God.
As regards the present question, I am willing to accept the unfavourable conditions which the prejudice assigns to me. I
consent that established custom, and the general feeling, should
be deemed conclusive against me, unless that custom and feeling
from age to age can be shown to have owed their existence to
other causes than their soundness, and to have derived their
power from the worse rather than the better parts of human
nature. I am willing that judgment should go against me, unless I can show that my judge has been tampered with. The
concession is not so great as it might appear ; for to prove this
is by far the easiest portion of my task.

5. The generality of a practice is in some cases a strong presumption that it is, or at all events once was, conducive to laud-
able ends. This is the case, when the practice was first adopted,
or afterwards kept up, as a means to such ends, and was
grounded on experience of the mode in which they could be
most effectually attained. If the authority of men over women,
when first established, had been the result of a conscientious
comparison between different modes of constituting the government of society ; if, after trying various other modes of social
organization—the government of women over men, equality
between the two, and such mixed and divided modes of government as might be invented—it had been decided, on the testimony of experience, that the mode in which women are wholly
under the rule of men, having no share at all in public concerns, and each in private being under the legal obligation of
obedience to the man with whom she has associated her
destiny, was the arrangement most conducive to the happiness
and well-being of both ; its general adoption might then be
fairly thought to be some evidence that, at the time when it
was adopted, it was the best : though even then the considerations which recommended it may, like so many other primeval
social facts of the greatest importance, have subsequently, in
the course of ages, ceased to exist. But the state of the case is
in every respect the reverse of this. In the first place, the
opinion in favour of the present system, which entirely subordinates the weaker sex to the stronger, rests upon theory

only; for there never has been trial made of any other: so that experience, in the sense in which it is vulgarly opposed to theory, cannot be pretended to have pronounced any verdict. And in the second place, the adoption of this system of inequality never was the result of deliberation, or forethought, or any social ideas, or any notion whatever of what conduced to the benefit of humanity or the good order of society. It arose simply from the fact that from the very earliest twilight of human society, every woman (owing to the value attached to her by men, combined with her inferiority in muscular strength) was found in a state of bondage to some man. Laws and systems of polity always begin by recognizing the relations they find already existing between individuals. They convert what was a mere physical fact into a legal right, give it the sanction of society, and principally aim at the substitution of public and organized means of asserting and protecting these rights, instead of the irregular and lawless conflict of physical strength. Those who had already been compelled to obedience became in this manner legally bound to it. Slavery, from being a mere affair of force between the master and the slave, became regularized and a matter of compact among the masters, who, binding themselves to one another for common protection, guaranteed by their collective strength the private possessions of each, including his slaves. In early times, the great majority of the male sex were slaves, as well as the whole of the female. And many ages elapsed, some of them ages of high cultivation, before any thinker was bold enough to question the rightfulness, and the absolute social necessity, either of the one slavery or of the other. By degrees such thinkers did arise: and (the general progress of society assisting) the slavery of the male sex has, in all the countries of Christian Europe at least (though, in one of them, only within the last few years), been at length abolished, and that of the female sex has been gradually changed into a milder form of dependence. But this dependence, as it exists at present, is not an original institution, taking a fresh start from considerations of justice and social expediency—it is the primitive state of slavery lasting on, through successive mitigations and modifications occasioned by the same causes which have softened the general manners, and brought all human relations more under the control of justice and the influence of humanity. It has not lost the taint of its brutal origin. No presumption in its favour, there-

fore, can be drawn from the fact of its existence. The only
such presumption which it could be supposed to have, must be
grounded on its having lasted till now, when so many other
things which came down from the same odious source have
been done away with. And this, indeed, is what makes it
strange to ordinary ears, to hear it asserted that the inequality
of rights between men and women has no other source than
the law of the strongest.

6. That this statement should have the effect of a paradox is
in some respects creditable to the progress of civilization, and
the improvement of the moral sentiments of mankind. We now
live—that is to say, one or two of the most advanced nations of
the world now live—in a state in which the law of the strongest
seems to be entirely abandoned as the regulating principle of
the world's affairs: nobody professes it, and, as regards most of
the relations between human beings, nobody is permitted to
practise it. When anyone succeeds in doing so, it is under
cover of some pretext which gives him the semblance of having
some general social interest on his side. This being the ostensible
state of things, people flatter themselves that the rule of mere
force is ended; that the law of the strongest cannot be the
reason of existence of anything which has remained in full
operation down to the present time. However any of our
present institutions may have begun, it can only, they think,
have been preserved to this period of advanced civilization by a
well-grounded feeling of its adaptation to human nature, and
conduciveness to the general good. They do not understand
the great vitality and durability of institutions which place right
on the side of might; how intensely they are clung to; how the
good as well as the bad propensities and sentiments of those
who have power in their hands, become identified with retaining
it; how slowly these bad institutions give way, one at a time,
the weakest first, beginning with those which are least inter-
woven with the daily habits of life; and how very rarely those
who have obtained legal power because they first had physical,
have ever lost their hold of the former until the physical power
had passed over to the other side. Such shifting of the physical
force not having taken place in the case of women; this fact,
combined with all the peculiar and characteristic features of the
particular case, made it certain from the first that this branch
of the system of right founded on might, though softened in its
most atrocious features at an earlier period than several of the

others, would be the very last to disappear. It was inevitable that this one case of a social relation grounded on force would survive through generations of institutions grounded on equal justice, an almost solitary exception to the general character of their laws and customs; but which, so long as it does not proclaim its own origin, and as discussion has not brought out its true character, is not felt to jar with modern civilization, any more than domestic slavery among the Greeks jarred with their notion of themselves as a free people.

7. The truth is, that people of the present and the last two or three generations have lost all practical sense of the primitive condition of humanity; and only the few who have studied history accurately, or have much frequented the parts of the world occupied by the living representatives of ages long past, are able to form any mental picture of what society then was. People are not aware how entirely, in former ages, the law of superior strength was the rule of life; how publicly and openly it was avowed. I do not say cynically or shamelessly—for these words imply a feeling that there was something in it to be ashamed of, and no such notion could find a place in the faculties of any person in those ages, except a philosopher or a saint. History gives a cruel experience of human nature, in showing how exactly the regard due to the life, possessions, and entire earthly happiness of any class of persons was measured by what they had the power of enforcing; how all who made any resistance to authorities that had arms in their hands, however dreadful might be the provocation, had not only the law of force but all other laws, and all the notions of social obligation against them; and, in the eyes of those whom they resisted, were not only guilty of crime, but of the worst of all crimes, deserving the most cruel chastisement which human beings could inflict. The first small vestige of a feeling of obligation in a superior to acknowledge any right in inferiors began when he had been induced, for convenience, to make some promise to them. Though these promises, even when sanctioned by the most solemn oaths, were for many ages revoked or violated on the most trifling provocation or temptation, it is probable that this, except by persons of still worse than the average morality, was seldom done without some twinges of conscience. The ancient republics, being mostly grounded from the first upon some kind of mutual compact, or at any rate formed by an union of persons not very unequal in strength, afforded, in consequence, the first

instance of a portion of human relations fenced round, and placed under the dominion of another law than that of force. And though the original law of force remained in full operation between them and their slaves, and also (except so far as limited by express compact) between a commonwealth and its subjects, or other independent commonwealths; the banishment of that primitive law, even from so narrow a field, commenced the regeneration of human nature, by giving birth to sentiments of which experience soon demonstrated the immense value even for material interests, and which thenceforward only required to be enlarged, not created. Though slaves were no part of the commonwealth, it was in the free states that slaves were first felt to have rights as human beings. The Stoics were, I believe, the first (except so far as the Jewish Law constitutes an exception) who taught as a part of morality that men were bound by moral obligations to their slaves. No one, after Christianity became ascendant, could ever again have been a stranger to this belief, in theory; nor, after the rise of the Catholic Church, was it ever without persons to stand up for it. Yet to enforce it was the most arduous task which Christianity ever had to perform. For more than a thousand years the Church kept up the contest, with hardly any perceptible success. It was not for want of power over men's minds. Its power was prodigious. It could make kings and nobles resign their most valued possessions to enrich the Church. It could make thousands, in the prime of life and the height of worldly advantages, shut themselves up in the convents to work out their salvation by poverty, fasting, and prayer. It could send hundreds of thousands across land and sea, Europe and Asia, to give their lives for the deliverance of the Holy Sepulchre. It could make kings relinquish wives who were the objects of their passionate attachment, because the Church declared that they were within the seventh (by our calculation the fourteenth) degree of relationship. All this it did; but it could not make men fight less with one another, nor tyrannize less cruelly over the serfs, and, when they were able, over burgesses. It could not make them renounce either of the applications of force; force militant; or force triumphant. This they could never be induced to do until they were themselves in their turn compelled by superior force. Only by the growing power of kings was an end put to fighting except between kings, or competitors for kingship; only by the growth of a wealthy and warlike bourgeoisie in the fortified towns, and of a plebeian infantry which proved more powerful in the field than the undisciplined chivalry, was the insolent tyranny of the nobles over the bourgeoisie and peasantry brought within some bounds. It was persisted in not only until, but long after, the oppressed had obtained a power enabling them often to take conspicuous vengeance; and on the Continent much of it continued to the time of the French Revolution, though in England the earlier and better organization of the democratic classes put an end to it sooner, by establishing equal laws and free national institutions.

8. If people are mostly so little aware how completely, during the greater part of the duration of our species, the law of force was the avowed rule of general conduct, any other being only a special and exceptional consequence of peculiar ties—and from how very recent a date it is that the affairs of society in general have been even pretended to be regulated according to any moral law; as little do people remember or consider how institutions and customs which never had any ground but the law of force last on into ages and states of general opinion which never would have permitted their first establishment. Less than forty years ago, Englishmen might still by law hold human beings in bondage as saleable property: within the present century they might kidnap them and carry them off, and work them literally to death. This absolutely extreme case of the law of force, condemned by those who can tolerate almost every other form of arbitrary power, and which, of all others, presents features the most revolting to the feelings of all who look at it from an impartial position, was the law of civilized and Christian England within the memory of persons now living: and in one half of Anglo-Saxon America, three or four years ago, not only did slavery exist, but the slave trade, and the breeding of slaves expressly for it, was a general practice between slave states. Yet not only was there a greater strength of sentiment against it, but, in England at least, a less amount either of feeling or of interest in favour of it, than of any other of the customary abuses of force: for its motive was the love of gain unmixed and undisguised; and those who profited by it were a very small numerical fraction of the country, while the natural feeling of all who were not personally interested in it was unmitigated abhorrence. So extreme an instance makes it almost superfluous to refer to any other: but consider the long duration of absolute monarchy. In England at present it is the almost

universal conviction that military despotism is a case of the law of force, having no other origin or justification. Yet in all the great nations of Europe except England it either still exists, or has only just ceased to exist, and has even now a strong party favourable to it in all ranks of the people, especially among persons of station and consequence. Such is the power of an established system, even when far from universal; when not only in almost every period of history there have been great and well-known examples of the contrary system, but these have almost invariably been afforded by the most illustrious and most prosperous communities. In this case, too, the possessor of the undue power, the person directly interested in it, is only one person, while those who are subject to it and suffer from it are literally all the rest. The yoke is naturally and necessarily humiliating to all persons, except the one who is on the throne, together with, at most, the one who expects to succeed to it. How different are these cases from that of the power of men over women! I am not now prejudging the question of its justifiableness. I am showing how vastly more permanent it could not but be, even if not justifiable, than these other dominations, which have nevertheless lasted down to our own time. Whatever gratification of pride there is in the possession of power, and whatever personal interest in its exercise, is in this case not confined to a limited class, but common to the whole male sex. Instead of being, to most of its supporters, a thing desirable chiefly in the abstract, or, like the political ends usually contended for by factions, of little private importance to any but the leaders; it comes home to the person and hearth of every male head of a family, and of every one who looks forward to being so. The clodhopper exercises, or is to exercise, his share of the power equally with the highest nobleman. And the case is that in which the desire of power is the strongest : for every one who desires power, desires it most over those who are nearest to him, with whom his life is passed, with whom he has most concerns in common, and in whom any independence of his authority is oftenest likely to interfere with his individual preferences. If, in the other cases specified, powers manifestly grounded only on force, and having so much less to support them, are so slowly and with so much difficulty got rid of, much more must it be so with this, even if it rests on no better foundation than those. We must consider, too, that the possessors of the power have facilities in this case, greater than in any other, to prevent any uprising against it. Every one of the subjects lives under the very eye, and almost, it may be said, in the hands, of one of the masters—in closer intimacy with him than with any of her fellow-subjects; with no means of combining against him, no power of even locally overmastering him, and, on the other hand, with the strongest motives for seeking his favour and avoiding to give him offence. In struggles for political emancipation, everybody knows how often its champions are bought off by bribes, or daunted by terrors. In the case of women, each individual of the subject-class is in a chronic state of bribery and intimidation combined. In setting up the standard of resistance, a large number of the leaders, and still more of the followers, must make an almost complete sacrifice of the pleasures or the alleviations of their own individual lot. If ever any system of privilege and enforced subjection had its yoke tightly riveted on the necks of those who are kept down by it, this has. I have not yet shown that it is a wrong system: but every one who is capable of thinking on the subject must see that, even if it is, it was certain to outlast all other forms of unjust authority. And when some of the grossest of the other forms still exist in many civilized countries, and have only recently been got rid of in others, it would be strange if that which is so much the deepest-rooted had yet been perceptibly shaken anywhere. There is more reason to wonder that the protests and testimonies against it should have been so numerous and so weighty as they are.

9. Some will object, that a comparison cannot fairly be made between the government of the male sex and the forms of unjust power which I have adduced in illustration of it, since these are arbitrary, and the effect of mere usurpation, while it on the contrary is natural. But was there ever any domination which did not appear natural to those who possessed it? There was a time when the division of mankind into two classes, a small one of masters and a numerous one of slaves, appeared, even to the most cultivated minds, to be a natural, and the only natural, condition of the human race. No less an intellect, and one which contributed no less to the progress of human thought, than Aristotle, held this opinion without doubt or misgiving; and rested it on the same premises on which the same assertion in regard to the dominion of men over women is usually based, namely that there are different natures among mankind, free

natures and slave natures; that the Greeks were of a free
nature, the barbarian races of Thracians and Asiatics of a slave
nature. But why need I go back to Aristotle? Did not the
slave-owners of the Southern United States maintain the same
doctrine, with all the fanaticism with which men cling to the
theories that justify their passions and legitimate their personal
interests? Did they not call heaven and earth to witness that
the dominion of the white man over the black is natural, that
the black race is by nature incapable of freedom, and marked
out for slavery?—some even going so far as to say that the freedom of manual labourers is an unnatural order of things anywhere. Again, the theorists of absolute monarchy have always
affirmed it to be the only natural form of government; issuing
from the patriarchal, which was the primitive and spontaneous
form of society, framed on the model of the paternal, which is
anterior to society itself, and, as they contend, the most natural
authority of all. Nay, for that matter, the law of force itself,
to those who could not plead any other, has always seemed the
most natural of all grounds for the exercise of authority. Conquering races hold it to be Nature's own dictate that the conquered should obey the conquerors, or, as they euphoniously
paraphrase it, that the feebler and more unwarlike races should
submit to the braver and manlier. The smallest acquaintance
with human life in the Middle Ages shows how supremely
natural the dominion of the feudal nobility over men of low
condition appeared to the nobility themselves, and how unnatural the conception seemed, of a person of the inferior class
claiming equality with them, or exercising authority over them.
It hardly seemed less so to the class held in subjection. The
emancipated serfs and burgesses, even in their most vigorous
struggles, never made any pretension to a share of authority;
they only demanded more or less of limitation to the power of
tyrannizing over them. So true is it that unnatural generally
means only uncustomary, and that everything which is usual
appears natural. The subjection of women to men being
a universal custom, any departure from it quite naturally appears
unnatural. But how entirely, even in this case, the feeling is
dependent on custom, appears by ample experience. Nothing
so much astonishes the people of distant parts of the world,
when they first learn anything about England, as to be told that
it is under a queen; the thing seems to them so unnatural as to
be almost incredible. To Englishmen this does not seem in the

least degree unnatural, because they are used to it; but they do feel it unnatural that women should be soldiers or members of parliament.   In the feudal ages, on the contrary, war and politics were not thought unnatural to women, because not unusual; it seemed natural that women of the privileged classes should be of manly character, inferior in nothing but bodily strength to their husbands and fathers.   The independence of women seemed rather less unnatural to the Greeks than to other ancients, on account of the fabulous Amazons (whom they believed to be historical), and the partial example afforded by the Spartan women; who, though no less subordinate by law thán in other Greek states, were more free in fact, and, being trained to bodily exercises in the same manner with men, gave ample proof that they were not naturally disqualified for them. There can be little doubt that Spartan experience suggested to Plato, among many other of his doctrines, that of the social and political equality of the two sexes.

10.   But, it will be said, the rule of men over women differs from all these others in not being a rule of force : it is accepted voluntarily; women make no complaint, and are consenting parties to it.   In the first place, a great number of women do not accept it.   Ever since there have been women able to make their sentiments known by their writings (the only mode of publicity which society permits to them), an increasing number of them have recorded protests against their present social condition : and recently many thousands of them, headed by the most eminent women known to the public, have petitioned Parliament for their admission to the parliamentary suffrage. The claim of women to be educated as solidly, and in the same branches of knowledge, as men, is urged with growing intensity, and with a great prospect of success; while the demand for their admission into professions and occupations hitherto closed against them becomes every year more urgent.   Though there are not in this country, as there are in the United States, periodical Conventions and an organized party to agitate for the Rights of Women, there is a numerous and active Society organized and managed by women, for the more limited object of obtaining the political franchise.   Nor is it only in our own country and in America that women are beginning to protest, more or less collectively, against the disabilities under which they labour.   France, and Italy, and Switzerland, and Russia now afford examples of the same thing.   How many more

women there are who silently cherish similar aspirations, no one can possibly know; but there are abundant tokens how many *would* cherish them, were they not so strenuously taught to repress them as contrary to the proprieties of their sex. It must be remembered, also, that no enslaved class ever asked for complete liberty at once. When Simon de Montfort called the deputies of the commons to sit for the first time in Parliament, did any of them dream of demanding that an assembly, elected by their constituents, should make and destroy ministries, and dictate to the king in affairs of state? No such thought entered into the imagination of the most ambitious of them. The nobility had already these pretensions; the commons pretended to nothing but to be exempt from arbitrary taxation, and from the gross individual oppression of the king's officers. It is a political law of nature that those who are under any power of ancient origin never begin by complaining of the power itself, but only of its oppressive exercise. There is never any want of women who complain of ill usage by their husbands. There would be infinitely more, if complaint were not the greatest of all provocatives to a repetition and increase of the ill usage. It is this which frustrates all attempts to maintain the power but protect the woman against its abuses. In no other case (except that of a child) is the person who has been proved judicially to have suffered an injury replaced under the physical power of the culprit who inflicted it. Accordingly wives, even in the most extreme and protracted cases of bodily ill usage, hardly ever dare avail themselves of the laws made for their protection: and if, in a moment of irrepressible indignation, or by the interference of neighbours, they are induced to do so, their whole effort afterwards is to disclose as little as they can, and to beg off their tyrant from his merited chastisement.

11. All causes, social and natural, combine to make it unlikely that women should be collectively rebellious to the power of men. They are so far in a position different from all other subject classes, that their masters require something more from them than actual service. Men do not want solely the obedience of women, they want their sentiments. All men, except the most brutish, desire to have, in the woman most nearly connected with them, not a forced slave but a willing one; not a slave merely, but a favourite. They have therefore put everything in practice to enslave their minds. The masters of all other slaves rely, for maintaining obedience, on fear; either fear of

themselves, or religious fears. The masters of women wanted
more than simple obedience, and they turned the whole force
of education to effect their purpose. All women are brought
up from the very earliest years in the belief that their ideal of
character is the very opposite to that of men ; not self-will, and
government by self-control, but submission, and yielding to the
control of others. All the moralities tell them that it is the
duty of women, and all the current sentimentalities that it is
their nature, to live for others ; to make complete abnegation of
themselves, and to have no life but in their affections. And by
their affections are meant the only ones they are allowed to
have—those to the men with whom they are connected, or to
the children who constitute an additional and indefeasible tie
between them and a man. When we put together three things
—first, the natural attraction between opposite sexes ; secondly,
the wife's entire dependence on the husband, every privilege or
pleasure she has being either his gift, or depending entirely on
his will ; and lastly, that the principal object of human pursuit,
consideration, and all objects of social ambition, can in general
be sought or obtained by her only through him—it would
be a miracle if the object of being attractive to men had
not become the polar star of feminine education and formation of character. And, this great means of influence over
the minds of women having been acquired, an instinct of
selfishness made men avail themselves of it to the utmost
as a means of holding women in subjection, by representing
to them meekness, submissiveness, and resignation of all
individual will into the hands of a man, as an essential part of
sexual attractiveness. Can it be doubted that any of the other
yokes which mankind have succeeded in breaking would have
subsisted till now if the same means had existed, and had been
as sedulously used to bow down their minds to it ? If it had
been made the object of the life of every young plebeian to find
personal favour in the eyes of some patrician, of every young
serf with some seigneur ; if domestication with him, and a share
of his personal affections, had been held out as the prize which
they all should look out for, the most gifted and aspiring being
able to reckon on the most desirable prizes ; and if, when this
prize had been obtained, they had been shut out by a wall of
brass from all interests not centring in him, all feelings and
desires but those which he shared or inculcated ; would not
serfs and seigneurs, plebeians and patricians, have been as

broadly distinguished at this day as men and women are? And would not all but a thinker here and there have believed the distinction to be a fundamental and unalterable fact in human nature?

12. The preceding considerations are amply sufficient to show that custom, however universal it may be, affords in this case no presumption, and ought not to create any prejudice, in favour of the arrangements which place women in social and political subjection to men. But I may go farther, and maintain that the course of history, and the tendencies of progressive human society, afford not only no presumption in favour of this system of inequality of rights, but a strong one against it; and that, so far as the whole course of human improvement up to this time, the whole stream of modern tendencies, warrants any inference on the subject, it is, that this relic of the past is discordant with the future, and must necessarily disappear.

13. For what is the peculiar character of the modern world —the difference which chiefly distinguishes modern institutions, modern social ideas, modern life itself, from those of times long past? It is, that human beings are no longer born to their place in life, and chained down by an inexorable bond to the place they are born to, but are free to employ their faculties, and such favourable chances as offer, to achieve the lot which may appear to them most desirable. Human society of old was constituted on a very different principle. All were born to a fixed social position, and were mostly kept in it by law, or interdicted from any means by which they could emerge from it. As some men are born white and others black, so some were born slaves and others freemen and citizens; some were born patricians, others plebeians; some were born feudal nobles, others commoners and *roturiers*. A slave or serf could never make himself free, nor, except by the will of his master, become so. In most European countries it was not till towards the close of the Middle Ages, and as a consequence of the growth of regal power, that commoners could be ennobled. Even among nobles, the eldest son was born the exclusive heir to the paternal possessions, and a long time elapsed before it was fully established that the father could disinherit him. Among the industrious classes, only those who were born members of a guild, or were admitted into it by its members, could lawfully practise their calling within its local limits; and nobody could practise any calling deemed important, in any but the legal

manner — by processes authoritatively prescribed. Manufacturers have stood in the pillory for presuming to carry on their
business by new and improved methods. In modern Europe,
and most in those parts of it which have participated most
largely in all other modern improvements, diametrically opposite doctrines now prevail. Law and government do not undertake to prescribe by whom any social or industrial operation
shall or shall not be conducted, or what modes of conducting
them shall be lawful. These things are left to the unfettered
choice of individuals. Even the laws which required that workmen should serve an apprenticeship have in this country been
repealed : there being ample assurance that in all cases in
which an apprenticeship is necessary, its necessity will suffice to
enforce it. The old theory was, that the least possible should
be left to the choice of the individual agent; that all he had to
do should, as far as practicable, be laid down for him by
superior wisdom. Left to himself he was sure to go wrong.
The modern conviction, the fruit of a thousand years of experience, is, that things in which the individual is the person
directly interested never go right but as they are left to his
own discretion; and that any regulation of them by authority,
except to protect the rights of others, is sure to be mischievous.
This conclusion, slowly arrived at, and not adopted until almost
every possible application of the contrary theory had been
made with disastrous result, now (in the industrial department)
prevails universally in the most advanced countries, almost
universally in all that have pretensions to any sort of advancement. It is not that all processes are supposed to be equally
good, or all persons to be equally qualified for everything; but that freedom of individual choice is now known
to be the only thing which procures the adoption of the
best processes, and throws each operation into the hands of
those who are best qualified for it. Nobody thinks it necessary to make a law that only a strong-armed man shall be
a blacksmith. Freedom and competition suffice to make black-
smiths strong-armed men, because the weak-armed can earn
more by engaging in occupations for which they are more fit.
In consonance with this doctrine, it is felt to be an overstep-
ping of the proper bounds of authority to fix beforehand, on
some general presumption, that certain persons are not fit to
do certain things. It is now thoroughly known and admitted
that if some such presumptions exist, no such presumption is

infallible. Even if it be well grounded in a majority of cases, which it is very likely not to be, there will be a minority of exceptional cases in which it does not hold: and in those it is both an injustice to the individuals, and a detriment to society, to place barriers in the way of their using their faculties for their own benefit and for that of others. In the cases, on the other hand, in which the unfitness is real, the ordinary motives of human conduct will on the whole suffice to prevent the incompetent person from making, or from persisting in, the attempt.

14. If this general principle of social and economical science is not true; if individuals, with such help as they can derive from the opinion of those who know them, are not better judges than the law and the government of their own capacities and vocation; the world cannot too soon abandon this principle, and return to the old system of regulations and disabilities. But if the principle is true, we ought to act as if we believed it, and not to ordain that to be born a girl instead of a boy, any more than to be born black instead of white, or a commoner instead of a nobleman, shall decide the person's position through all life—shall interdict people from all the more elevated social positions, and from all, except a few, respectable occupations. Even were we to admit the utmost that is ever pretended as to the superior fitness of men for all the functions now reserved to them, the same argument applies which forbids a legal qualification for members of Parliament. If only once in a dozen years the conditions of eligibility exclude a fit person, there is a real loss, while the exclusion of thousands of unfit persons is no gain; for if the constitution of the electoral body disposes them to choose unfit persons, there are always plenty of such persons to choose from. In all things of any difficulty and importance, those who can do them well are fewer than the need, even with the most unrestricted latitude of choice: and any limitation of the field of selection deprives society of some chances of being served by the competent, without ever saving it from the incompetent.

15. At present, in the more improved countries, the disabilities of women are the only case, save one, in which laws and institutions take persons at their birth, and ordain that they shall never in all their lives be allowed to compete for certain things. The one exception is that of royalty. Persons still are born to the throne; no one, not of the reigning family, can

ever occupy it, and no one even of that family can, by any
means but the course of hereditary succession, attain it. All
other dignities and social advantages are open to the whole
male sex: many indeed are only attainable by wealth, but
wealth may be striven for by anyone, and is actually obtained
by many men of the very humblest origin. The difficulties, to
the majority, are indeed insuperable without the aid of fortunate
accidents; but no male human being is under any legal ban :
neither law nor opinion superadd artificial obstacles to the natural
ones. Royalty, as I have said, is excepted : but in this case
everyone feels it to be an exception—an anomaly in the modern
world, in marked opposition to its customs and principles, and
to be justified only by extraordinary special expediences, which,
though individuals and nations differ in estimating their weight,
unquestionably do in fact exist. But in this exceptional case,
in which a high social function is, for important reasons, be-
stowed on birth instead of being put up to competition, all free
nations contrive to adhere in substance to the principle from
which they nominally derogate; for they circumscribe this high
function by conditions avowedly intended to prevent the person
to whom it ostensibly belongs from really performing it; while
the person by whom it is performed, the responsible minister,
does obtain the post by a competition from which no full-grown
citizen of the male sex is legally excluded. The disabilities,
therefore, to which women are subject from the mere fact of
their birth, are the solitary examples of the kind in modern
legislation. In no instance except this, which comprehends
half the human race, are the higher social functions closed
against anyone by a fatality of birth which no exertions, and
no change of circumstances, can overcome; for even religious
disabilities (besides that in England and in Europe they have
practically almost ceased to exist) do not close any career to the
disqualified person in case of conversion.

16. The social subordination of women thus stands out an
isolated fact in modern social institutions; a solitary breach of
what has become their fundamental law; a single relic of an
old world of thought and practice exploded in everything else,
but retained in the one thing of most universal interest; as if a
gigantic dolmen, or a vast temple of Jupiter Olympius, occupied
the site of St. Paul's and received daily worship, while the sur-
rounding Christian churches were only resorted to on fasts and
festivals. This entire discrepancy between one social fact and

all those which accompany it, and the radical opposition between its nature and the progressive movement which is the boast of the modern world, and which has successively swept away everything else of an analogous character, surely affords, to a conscientious observer of human tendencies, serious matter for reflection. It raises a primâ facie presumption on the unfavourable side, far outweighing any which custom and usage could in such circumstances create on the favourable; and should at least suffice to make this, like the choice between republicanism and royalty, a balanced question.

17. The least that can be demanded is, that the question should not be considered as prejudged by existing fact and existing opinion, but open to discussion on its merits, as a question of justice and expediency: the decision on this, as on any of the other social arrangements of mankind, depending on what an enlightened estimate of tendencies and consequences may show to be most advantageous to humanity in general, without distinction of sex. And the discussion must be a real discussion, descending to foundations, and not resting satisfied with vague and general assertions. It will not do, for instance, to assert in general terms that the experience of mankind has pronounced in favour of the existing system. Experience cannot possibly have decided between two courses, so long as there has only been experience of one. If it be said that the doctrine of the equality of the sexes rests only on theory, it must be remembered that the contrary doctrine also has only theory to rest upon. All that is proved in its favour by direct experience is that mankind have been able to exist under it, and to attain the degree of improvement and prosperity which we now see; but whether that prosperity has been attained sooner, or is now greater, than it would have been under the other system, experience does not say. On the other hand, experience does say that every step in improvement has been so invariably accompanied by a step made in raising the social position of women, that historians and philosophers have been led to adopt their elevation or debasement as on the whole the surest test and most correct measure of the civilization of a people or an age. Through all the progressive period of human history, the condition of women has been approaching nearer to equality with men. This does not of itself prove that the assimilation must go on to complete equality; but it assuredly affords some presumption that such is the case.

18. Neither does it avail anything to say that the *nature* of the two sexes adapts them to their present functions and position, and renders these appropriate to them. Standing on the ground of common sense and the constitution of the human mind, I deny that anyone knows, or can know, the nature of the two sexes, as long as they have only been seen in their present relation to one another. If men had ever been found in society without women, or women without men, or if there had been a society of men and women in which the women were not under the control of the men, something might have been positively known about the mental and moral differences which may be inherent in the nature of each. What is now called the nature of women is an eminently artificial thing—the result of forced repression in some directions, unnatural stimulation in others. It may be asserted, without scruple, that no other class of dependents have had their character so entirely distorted from its natural proportions by their relations with their masters; for, if conquered and slave races have been, in some respects, more forcibly repressed, whatever in them has not been crushed down by an iron heel has generally been let alone, and if left with any liberty of development, it has developed itself according to its own laws; but in the case of women, a hot-house and stove cultivation has always been carried on of some of the capabilities of their nature, for the benefit and pleasure of their masters. Then, because certain products of the general vital force sprout luxuriantly and reach a great development in this heated atmosphere and under this active nurture and watering, while other shoots from the same root, which are left outside in the wintry air, with ice purposely heaped all round them, have a stunted growth, and some are burnt off with fire and disappear; men, with that inability to recognize their own work which distinguishes the unanalytic mind, indolently believe that the tree grows of itself in the way they have made it grow, and that it would die if one half of it were not kept in a vapour bath and the other half in the snow.

19. Of all difficulties which impede the progress of thought, and the formation of well-grounded opinions on life and social arrangements, the greatest is now the unspeakable ignorance and inattention of mankind in respect to the influences which form human character. Whatever any portion of the human species now are, or seem to be, such, it is supposed, they have a natural tendency to be; even when the most elementary

knowledge of the circumstances in which they have been placed, clearly points out the causes that made them what they are. Because a cottier deeply in arrears to his landlord is not industrious, there are people who think that the Irish are naturally idle. Because constitutions can be overthrown when the authorities appointed to execute them turn their arms against them, there are people who think the French incapable of free government. Because the Greeks cheated the Turks, and the Turks only plundered the Greeks, there are persons who think that the Turks are naturally more sincere: and because women, as is often said, care nothing about politics except their personalities, it is supposed that the general good is naturally less interesting to women than to men. History, which is now so much better understood than formerly, teaches another lesson: if only by showing the extraordinary susceptibility of human nature to external influences, and the extreme variableness of those of its manifestations which are supposed to be most universal and uniform. But in history, as in travelling, men usually see only what they already had in their own minds; and few learn much from history who do not bring much with them to its study.

20. Hence, in regard to that most difficult question, what are the natural differences between the two sexes—a subject on which it is impossible in the present state of society to obtain complete and correct knowledge—while almost everybody dogmatizes upon it, almost all neglect and make light of the only means by which any partial insight can be obtained into it. This is an analytic study of the most important department of psychology, the laws of the influence of circumstances on character. For, however great and apparently ineradicable the moral and intellectual differences between men and women might be, the evidence of their being natural differences could only be negative. Those only could be inferred to be natural which could not possibly be artificial—the residuum, after deducting every characteristic of either sex which can admit of being explained from education or external circumstances. The profoundest knowledge of the laws of the formation of character is indispensable to entitle anyone to affirm even that there is any difference, much more what the difference is, between the two sexes considered as moral and rational beings; and since no one, as yet, has that knowledge (for there is hardly any subject which, in proportion to its importance, has been so

little studied), no one is thus far entitled to any positive opinion on the subject. Conjectures are all that can at present be made ; conjectures more or less probable, according as more or less authorized by such knowledge as we yet have of the laws of psychology, as applied to the formation of character.

21. Even ¦the preliminary knowledge, what the differences between the sexes now are, apart from all question as to how they are made what they are, is still in the crudest and most incomplete state. Medical practitioners and physiologists have ascertained, to some extent, the differences in bodily constitution ; and this is an important element to the psychologist. But hardly any medical practitioner is a psychologist. Respecting the mental characteristics of women, their observations are of no more worth than those of common men. It is a subject on which nothing final can be known, so long as those who alone can really know it—women themselves—have given but little testimony, and that little mostly suborned. It is easy to know stupid women. Stupidity is much the same all the world over. A stupid person's notions and feelings may confidently be inferred from those which prevail in the circle by which the person is surrounded. Not so with those whose opinions and feelings are an emanation from their own nature and faculties. It is only a man here and there who has any tolerable knowledge of the character even of the women of his own family. I do not mean of their capabilities ; these nobody knows, not even themselves, because most of them have never been called out. I mean their actually existing thoughts and feelings. Many a man thinks he perfectly understands women, because he has had amatory relations with several, perhaps with many of them. If he is a good observer, and his experience extends to quality as well as quantity, he may have learnt something of one narrow department of their nature—an important department, no doubt. But of all the rest of it, few persons are generally more ignorant, because there are few from whom it is so carefully hidden. The most favourable case which a man can generally have for studying the character of a woman is that of his own wife : for the opportunities are greater, and the cases of complete sympathy not so unspeakably rare. And, in fact, this is the source from which any knowledge worth having on the subject has, I believe, generally come. But most men have not had the opportunity of studying in this way more than a single case : accordingly one can, to an

almost laughable degree, infer what a man's wife is like, from
his opinions about women in general. To make even this one
case yield any result, the woman must be worth knowing, and
the man not only a competent judge, but of a character so
sympathetic in itself, and so well adapted to hers, that he can
either read her mind by sympathetic intuition, or has nothing
in himself which makes her shy of disclosing it. Hardly anything, I believe, can be more rare than this conjunction. It
often happens that there is the most complete unity of feeling
and community of interests as to all external things, yet the
one has as little admission into the internal life of the other as
if they were common acquaintance. Even with true affection,
authority on the one side and subordination on the other prevent perfect confidence. Though nothing may be intentionally
withheld, much is not shown. In the analogous relation of
parent and child, the corresponding phenomenon must have
been in the observation of every one. As between father and
son, how many are the cases in which the father, in spite of
real affection on both sides, obviously to all the world does not
know, nor suspect, parts of the son's character familiar to his
companions and equals. The truth is, that the position of looking up to another is extremely unpropitious to complete sincerity
and openness with him. The fear of losing ground in his opinion
or in his feelings is so strong that, even in an upright character,
there is an unconscious tendency to show only the best side, or
the side which, though not the best, is that which he most likes
to see: and it may be confidently said that thorough knowledge
of one another hardly ever exists but between persons who,
besides being intimates, are equals. How much more true,
then, must all this be, when the one is not only under the
authority of the other, but has it inculcated on her as a duty to
reckon everything else subordinate to his comfort and pleasure,
and to let him neither see nor feel anything coming from her,
except what is agreeable to him. All these difficulties stand in
the way of a man's obtaining any thorough knowledge even of
the one woman whom alone, in general, he has sufficient opportunity of studying. When we further consider that to understand one woman is not necessarily to understand any other
woman; that even if he could study many women of one rank,
or of one country, he would not thereby understand women of
other ranks or countries: and even if he did, they are still only
the women of a single period of history; we may safely assert

that the knowledge which men can acquire of women, even as they have been and are, without reference to what they might be, is wretchedly imperfect and superficial, and always will be so until women themselves have told all that they have to tell.

22. And this time has not come; nor will it come otherwise than gradually. It is but of yesterday that women have either been qualified by literary accomplishments, or permitted by society, to tell anything to the general public. As yet very few of them dare tell anything which men, on whom their literary success depends, are unwilling to hear. Let us remember in what manner, up to a very recent time, the expression, even by a male author, of uncustomary opinions, or what are deemed eccentric feelings, usually was, and in some degree still is, received; and we may form some faint conception under what impediments a woman, who is brought up to think custom and opinion her sovereign rule, attempts to express in books anything drawn from the depths of her own nature. The greatest woman who has left writings behind her sufficient to give her an eminent rank in the literature of her country, thought it necessary to prefix as a motto to her boldest work, "Un homme peut braver l'opinion ; une femme doit s'y soumettre."[1] The greater part of what women write about women is mere sycophancy to men. In the case of unmarried women, much of it seems only intended to increase their chance of a husband. Many, both married and unmarried, overstep the mark, and inculcate a servility beyond what is desired or relished by any man, except the very vulgarest. But this is not so often the case as, even at a quite late period, it still was. Literary women are becoming more freespoken, and more willing to express their real sentiments. Unfortunately, in this country especially, they are themselves such artificial products that their sentiments are compounded of a small element of individual observation and consciousness, and a very large one of acquired associations. This will be less and less the case, but it will remain true to a great extent, as long as social institutions do not admit the same free development of originality in women which is possible to men. When that time comes, and not before, we shall see, and not merely hear, as much as it is necessary to know of the nature of women, and the adaptation of other things to it.

23. I have dwelt so much on the difficulties which at present

---

[1] Title-page of Mme. de Staël's "Delphine."

obstruct any real knowledge by men of the true nature of women, because in this as in so many other things "opinio copiæ inter maximas causas inopiæ est;" and there is little chance of reasonable thinking on the matter, while people flatter themselves that they perfectly understand a subject of which most men know absolutely nothing, and of which it is at present impossible that any man, or all men taken together, should have knowledge which can qualify them to lay down the law to women as to what is, or is not, their vocation. Happily, no such knowledge is necessary for any practical purpose connected with the position of women in relation to society and life. For, according to all the principles involved in modern society, the question rests with women themselves—to be decided by their own experience, and by the use of their own faculties. There are no means of finding what either one person or many can do, but by trying—and no means by which anyone else can discover for them what it is for their happiness to do or leave undone.

24. One thing we may be certain of—that what is contrary to women's nature to do, they never will be made to do by simply giving their nature free play. The anxiety of mankind to interfere in behalf of nature, for fear lest nature should not succeed in effecting its purpose, is an altogether unnecessary solicitude. What women by nature cannot do, it is quite superfluous to forbid them from doing. What they can do, but not so well as the men who are their competitors, competition suffices to exclude them from; since nobody asks for protective duties and bounties in favour of women; it is only asked that the present bounties and protective duties in favour of men should be recalled. If women have a greater natural inclination for some things than for others, there is no need of laws or social inculcation to make the majority of them do the former in preference to the latter. Whatever women's services are most wanted for, the free play of competition will hold out the strongest inducements to them to undertake. And, as the words imply, they are most wanted for the things for which they are most fit; by the apportionment of which to them, the collective faculties of the two sexes can be applied on the whole with the greatest sum of valuable result.

25. The general opinion of men is supposed to be, that the natural vocation of a woman is that of a wife and mother. I say, is supposed to be, because, judging from acts—from

the whole of the present constitution of society—one might infer that their opinion was the direct contrary. They might be supposed to think that the alleged natural vocation of women was of all things the most repugnant to their nature; insomuch that if they are free to do anything else —if any other means of living, or occupation of their time and faculties, is open, which has any chance of appearing desirable to them—there will not be enough of them who will be willing to accept the condition said to be natural to them. If this is the real opinion of men in general, it would be well that it should be spoken out. I should like to hear somebody openly enunciating the doctrine (it is already implied in much that is written on the subject)—"It is necessary to society that women should marry and produce children. They will not do so unless they are compelled. Therefore it is necessary to compel them." The merits of the case would then be clearly defined. It would be exactly that of the slaveholders of South Carolina and Louisiana. "It is necessary that cotton and sugar should be grown. White men cannot produce them. Negroes will not, for any wages which we choose to give. *Ergo* they must be compelled." An illustration still closer to the point is that of impressment. Sailors must absolutely be had to defend the country. It often happens that they will not voluntarily enlist. Therefore there must be the power of forcing them. How often has this logic been used! and, but for one flaw in it, without doubt it would have been successful up to this day. But it is open to the retort—First pay the sailors the honest value of their labour. When you have made it as well worth their while to serve you as to work for other employers, you will have no more difficulty than others have in obtaining their services. To this there is no logical answer except "I will not :" and as people are now not only ashamed, but are not desirous, to rob the labourer of his hire, impressment is no longer advocated. Those who attempt to force women into marriage by closing all other doors against them, lay themselves open to a similar retort. If they mean what they say, their opinion must evidently be, that men do not render the married condition so desirable to women as to induce them to accept it for its own recommendations. It is not a sign of one's thinking the boon one offers very attractive, when one allows only Hobson's choice, "that or none." And here, I believe, is the clue to the feelings of those men who have a real antipathy

to the equal freedom of women. I believe they are afraid, not
lest women should be unwilling to marry, for I do not think that
anyone in reality has that apprehension; but lest they should
insist that marriage should be on equal conditions; lest all
women of spirit and capacity should prefer doing almost anything else, not in their own eyes degrading, rather than marry,
when marrying is giving themselves a master, and a master too
of all their earthly possessions. And truly, if this consequence
were necessarily incident to marriage, I think that the apprehension would be very well founded. I agree in thinking it
probable that few women, capable of anything else, would,
unless under an irresistible *entrainement*, rendering them for the
time insensible to anything but itself, choose such a lot, when
any other means were open to them of filling a conventionally
honourable place in life : and if men are determined that the
law of marriage shall be a law of despotism, they are quite
right, in point of mere policy, in leaving to women only Hobson's
choice.   But, in that case, all that has been done in the modern
world to. relax the chain on the minds of women has been a
mistake.   They never should have been allowed to receive a
literary education.   Women who read, much more women who
write, are, in the existing constitution of things, a contradiction
and a disturbing element : and it was wrong to bring women
up with any acquirements but those of an odalisque, or of a
domestic servant.

CHAPTER II

1. It will be well to commence the detailed discussion of the subject by the particular branch of it to which the course of our observations has led us: the conditions which the laws of this and all other countries annex to the marriage contract. Marriage being the destination appointed by society for women, the prospect they are brought up to, and the object which it is intended should be sought by all of them, except those who are too little attractive to be chosen by any man as his companion; one might have supposed that everything would have been done to make this condition as eligible to them as possible, that they might have no cause to regret being denied the option of any other. Society, however, both in this and, at first, in all other cases, has preferred to attain its object by foul rather than fair means: but this is the only case in which it has substantially persisted in them even to the present day. Originally women were taken by force, or regularly sold by their father to the husband. Until a late period in European history, the father had the power to dispose of his daughter in marriage at his own will and pleasure, without any regard to hers. The Church, indeed, was so far faithful to a better morality as to require a formal "yes" from the woman at the marriage ceremony; but there was nothing to show that the consent was other than compulsory; and it was practically impossible for the girl to refuse compliance if the father persevered, except perhaps when she might obtain the protection of religion by a determined resolution to take monastic vows. After marriage, the man had anciently (but this was anterior to Christianity) the power of life and death over his wife. She could invoke no law against him; he was her sole tribunal and law. For a long time he could repudiate her, but she had no corresponding power in regard to him. By the old laws of England, the husband was called the *lord* of the wife; he was literally regarded as her sovereign, inasmuch that the murder of a man by his wife was

35

called treason (*petty* as distinguished from *high* treason), and
was more cruelly avenged than was usually the case with
high treason, for the penalty was burning to death. Because
these various enormities have fallen into disuse (for most of
them were never formally abolished, or not until they had long
ceased to be practised) men suppose that all is now as it should be
in regard to the marriage contract; and we are continually told
that civilization and Christianity have restored to the woman her
just rights. Meanwhile the wife is the actual bond-servant
of her husband: no less so, as far as legal obligation goes, than
slaves commonly so called. She vows a lifelong obedience to
him at the altar, and is held to it all through her life by law.
Casuists may say that the obligation of obedience stops short
of participation in crime, but it certainly extends to everything
else. She can do no act whatever but by his permission, at
least tacit. She can acquire no property but for him; the
instant it becomes hers, even if by inheritance, it becomes *ipso
facto* his. In this respect the wife's position under the common
law of England is worse than that of slaves in the laws of many
countries: by the Roman law, for example, a slave might have
his peculium, which to a certain extent the law guaranteed
to him for his exclusive use. The higher classes in this country
have given an analogous advantage to their women, through
special contracts setting aside the law, by conditions of pin-
money, etc.; since, parental feeling being stronger with fathers
than the class feeling of their own sex, a father generally prefers
his own daughter to a son-in-law who is a stranger to him. By
means of settlements the rich usually contrive to withdraw the
whole or part of the inherited property of the wife from the
absolute control of the husband: but they do not succeed in
keeping it under her own control; the utmost they can do only
prevents the husband from squandering it, at the same time de-
barring the rightful owner from its use. The property itself is
out of the reach of both; and as to the income derived from
it, the form of settlement most favourable to the wife (that
called "to her separate use") only precludes the husband from
receiving it instead of her: it must pass through her hands, but
if he takes it from her by personal violence as soon as she
receives it, he can neither be punished nor compelled to
restitution. This is the amount of the protection which, under
the laws of this country, the most powerful nobleman can give
to his own daughter as respects her husband. In the immense

majority of cases there is no settlement: and the absorption of all rights, all property, as well as all freedom of action, is complete. The two are called "one person in law," for the purpose of inferring that whatever is hers is his, but the parallel inference is never drawn that whatever is his is hers; the maxim is not applied against the man, except to make him responsible to third parties for her acts, as a master is for the acts of his slaves or of his cattle. I am far from pretending that wives are in general no better treated than slaves; but no slave is a slave to the same lengths, and in so full a sense of the word, as a wife is. Hardly any slave, except one immediately attached to the master's person, is a slave at all hours and all minutes; in general he has, like a soldier, his fixed task, and when it is done, or when he is off duty, he disposes, within certain limits, of his own time, and has a family life into which the master rarely intrudes. "Uncle Tom" under his first master had his own life in his "cabin," almost as much as any man whose work takes him away from home is able to have in his own family. But it cannot be so with the wife. Above all, a female slave has (in Christian countries) an admitted right, and is considered under a moral obligation, to refuse to her master the last familiarity. Not so the wife: however brutal a tyrant she may unfortunately be chained to—though she may know that he hates her, though it may be his daily pleasure to torture her, and though she may feel it impossible not to loathe him—he can claim from her and enforce the lowest degradation of a human being, that of being made the instrument of an animal function contrary to her inclinations. While she is held in this worst description of slavery as to her own person, what is her position in regard to the children in whom she and her master have a joint interest? They are by law *his* children. He alone has any legal rights over them. Not one act can she do towards or in relation to them, except by delegation from him. Even after he is dead she is not their legal guardian, unless he by will has made her so. He could even send them away from her, and deprive her of the means of seeing or corresponding with them, until this power was in some degree restricted by Serjeant Talfourd's Act. This is her legal state. And from this state she has no means of withdrawing herself. If she leaves her husband, she can take nothing with her, neither her children nor anything which is rightfully her own. If he chooses, he can compel her to return, by law, or by physical force; or he may content himself with seizing for his own use anything which she may earn, or which may be given to her by her relations. It is only legal separation by a decree of a court of justice, which entitles her to live apart, without being forced back into the custody of an exasperated jailer—or which empowers her to apply any earnings to her own use, without fear that a man whom perhaps she has not seen for twenty years will pounce upon her some day and carry all off. This legal separation, until lately, the courts of justice would only give at an expense which made it inaccessible to any-one out of the higher ranks. Even now it is only given in cases of desertion, or of the extreme of cruelty; and yet complaints are made every day that it is granted too easily. Surely, if a woman is denied any lot in life but that of being the personal body-servant of a despot, and is dependent for everything upon the chance of finding one who may be disposed to make a favourite of her instead of merely a drudge, it is a very cruel aggravation of her fate that she should be allowed to try this chance only once. The natural sequel and corollary from this state of things would be, that since her all in life depends upon obtaining a good master, she should be allowed to change again and again until she finds one. I am not saying that she ought to be allowed this privilege. That is a totally different con-sideration. The question of divorce, in the sense involving liberty of remarriage, is one into which it is foreign to my pur-pose to enter. All I now say is, that to those to whom nothing but servitude is allowed, the free choice of servitude is the only, though a most insufficient, alleviation. Its refusal completes the assimilation of the wife to the slave—and the slave under not the mildest form of slavery: for in some slave codes the slave could, under certain circumstances of ill usage, legally compel the master to sell him. But no amount of ill usage, without adultery superadded, will in England free a wife from her tormentor.

2. I have no desire to exaggerate, nor does the case stand in any need of exaggeration. I have described the wife's legal position, not her actual treatment. The laws of most countries are far worse than the people who execute them, and many of them are only able to remain laws by being seldom or never carried into effect. If married life were all that it might be expected to be, looking to the laws alone, society would be a hell upon earth. Happily there are both feelings and interests

which in many men exclude, and in most greatly temper, the impulses and propensities which lead to tyranny: and of those feelings, the tie which connects a man with his wife affords, in a normal state of things, incomparably the strongest example. The only tie which at all approaches to it, that between him and his children, tends, in all save exceptional cases, to strengthen, instead of conflicting with, the first. Because this is true; because men in general do not inflict, nor women suffer, all the misery which could be inflicted and suffered if the full power of tyranny with which the man is legally invested were acted on; the defenders of the existing form of the institution think that all its iniquity is justified, and that any complaint is merely quarrelling with the evil which is the price paid for every great good. But the mitigations in practice, which are compatible with maintaining in full legal force this or any other kind of tyranny, instead of being any apology for despotism, only serve to prove what power human nature possesses of reacting against the vilest institutions, and with what vitality the seeds of good as well as those of evil in human character diffuse and propagate themselves. Not a word can be said for despotism in the family which cannot be said for political despotism. Every absolute king does not sit at his window to enjoy the groans of his tortured subjects, nor strips them of their last rag and turns them out to shiver in the road. The despotism of Louis XVI. was not the despotism of Philippe le Bel, or of Nadir Shah, or of Caligula; but it was bad enough to justify the French Revolution, and to palliate even its horrors. If an appeal be made to the intense attachments which exist between wives and their husbands, exactly as much may be said of domestic slavery. It was quite an ordinary fact in Greece and Rome for slaves to submit to death by torture rather than betray their masters. In the proscriptions of the Roman civil wars it was remarked that wives and slaves were heroically faithful, sons very commonly treacherous. Yet we know how cruelly many Romans treated their slaves. But in truth these intense individual feelings nowhere rise to such a luxuriant height as under the most atrocious institutions. It is part of the irony of life that the strongest feelings of devoted gratitude of which human nature seems to be susceptible, are called forth in human beings towards those who, having the power entirely to crush their earthly existence, voluntarily refrain from using that power. How great a place in most men this sentiment fills, even in religious devotion, it would be cruel to inquire. We daily see how much their gratitude to Heaven appears to be stimulated by the contemplation of fellow-creatures to whom God has not been so merciful as he has to themselves.

3. Whether the institution to be defended is slavery, political absolutism, or the absolutism of the head of a family, we are always expected to judge of it from its best instances; and we are presented with pictures of loving exercise of authority on one side, loving submission to it on the other—superior wisdom ordering all things for the greatest good of the dependents, and surrounded by their smiles and benedictions. All this would be very much to the purpose if anyone pretended that there are no such things as good men. Who doubts that there may be great goodness, and great happiness, and great affection, under the absolute government of a good man? Meanwhile, laws and institutions require to be adapted, not to good men, but to bad. Marriage is not an institution designed for a select few. Men are not required, as a preliminary to the marriage ceremony, to prove by testimonials that they are fit to be trusted with the exercise of absolute power. The tie of affection and obligation to a 'wife and children is very strong with those whose general social feelings are strong, and with many who are little sensible to any other social ties; but there are all degrees of sensibility and insensibility to it, as there are all grades of goodness and wickedness in men, down to those whom no ties will bind, and on whom society has no action but through its *ultima ratio*, the penalties of the law. In every grade of this descending scale are men to whom are committed all the legal powers of a husband. The vilest malefactor has some wretched woman tied to him, against whom he can commit any atrocity except killing her, and, if tolerably cautious, can do that without much danger of the legal penalty. And how many thousands are there among the lowest classes in every country, who, without being in a legal sense malefactors in any other respect, because in every other quarter their aggressions meet with resistance, indulge the utmost habitual excesses of bodily violence towards the unhappy wife, who alone, at least of grown persons, can neither repel nor escape from their brutality; and towards whom the excess of dependence inspires their mean and savage natures, not with a generous forbearance, and a point of honour to behave well to one whose lot in life is

trusted entirely to their kindness, but on the contrary with
a notion that the law has delivered her to them as their thing,
to be used at their pleasure, and that they are not expected to
practise the consideration towards her which is required from
them towards everybody else. The law, which till lately left
even these atrocious extremes of domestic oppression practically
unpunished, has within these few years made some feeble
attempts to repress them. But its attempts have done little,
and cannot be expected to do much, because it is contrary
to reason and experience to suppose that there can be any real
check to brutality, consistent with leaving the victim still in the
power of the executioner. Until a conviction for personal
violence, or at all events a repetition of it after the first conviction, entitles the woman *ipso facto* to a divorce, or at least to
a judicial separation, the attempt to repress these "aggravated
assaults" by legal penalties will break down for want of a
prosecutor, or for want of a witness.

4. When we consider how vast is the number of men, in any
great country, who are little higher than brutes, and that this
never prevents them from being able, through the law of
marriage, to obtain a victim, the breadth and depth of human
misery caused in this shape alone by the abuse of the institution
swells to something appalling. Yet these are only the extreme
cases. They are the lowest abysses, but there is a sad succession of depth after depth before reaching them. In domestic
as in political tyranny, the case of absolute monsters chiefly
illustrates the institution by showing that there is scarcely any
horror which may not occur under it if the despot pleases, and
thus setting in a strong light what must be the terrible fre-
quency of things only a little less atrocious. Absolute fiends
are as rare as angels, perhaps rarer: ferocious savages, with
occasional touches of humanity, are however very frequent:
and in the wide interval which separates these from any worthy
representatives of the human species, how many are the forms
and gradations of animalism and selfishness, often under an
outward varnish of civilization and even cultivation, living at
peace with the law, maintaining a creditable appearance to
all who are not under their power, yet sufficient often to make
the lives of all who are so, a torment and a burthen to them!
It would be tiresome to repeat the commonplaces about the unfitness of men in general for power, which, after the political
discussions of centuries, every one knows by heart, were it not

that hardly anyone thinks of applying these maxims to the case in which above all others they are applicable, that of power, not placed in the hands of a man here and there, but offered to every adult male, down to the basest and most ferocious. It is not because a man is not known to have broken any of the Ten Commandments, or because he maintains a respectable character in his dealings with those whom he cannot compel to have intercourse with him, or because he does not fly out into violent bursts of ill-temper against those who are not obliged to bear with him, that it is possible to surmise of what sort his conduct will be in the unrestraint of home. Even the commonest men reserve the violent, the sulky, the undisguisedly selfish side of their character for those who have no power to withstand it. The relation of superiors to dependents is the nursery of these vices of character, which, wherever else they exist, are an overflowing from that source. A man who is morose or violent to his equals, is sure to be one who has lived among inferiors, whom he could frighten or worry into submission. If the family in its best forms is, as it is often said to be, a school of sympathy, tenderness, and loving forgetfulness of self, it is still oftener, as respects its chief, a school of wilfulness, overbearingness, unbounded selfish indulgence, and a double-dyed and idealized selfishness, of which sacrifice itself is only a particular form: the care for the wife and children being only care for them as parts of the man's own interests and belongings, and their individual happiness being immolated in every shape to his smallest preferences. What better is to be looked for under the existing form of the institution? We know that the bad propensities of human nature are only kept within bounds when they are allowed no scope for their indulgence. We know that from impulse and habit, when not from deliberate purpose, almost every one to whom others yield goes on encroaching upon them, until a point is reached at which they are compelled to resist. Such being the common tendency of human nature, the almost unlimited power which present social institutions give to the man over at least one human being—the one with whom he resides, and whom he has always present—this power seeks out and evokes the latent germs of selfishness in the remotest corners of his nature—fans its faintest sparks and smouldering embers—offers to him a licence for the indulgence of those points of his original character which in all other relations he would have found it necessary to repress and conceal, and the repression of which would in time have become a second nature. I know that there is another side to the question. I grant that the wife, if she cannot effectually resist, can at least retaliate; she, too, can make the man's life extremely uncomfortable, and by that power is able to carry many points which she ought, and many which she ought not, to prevail in. But this instrument of self-protection—which may be called the power of the scold, or the shrewish sanction—has the fatal defect, that it avails most against the least tyrannical superiors, and in favour of the least deserving dependents. It is the weapon of irritable and self-willed women; of those who would make the worst use of power if they themselves had it, and who generally turn this power to a bad use. The amiable cannot use such an instrument, the high-minded disdain it. And on the other hand, the husbands against whom it is used most effectively are the gentler and more inoffensive; those who cannot be induced, even by provocation, to resort to any very harsh exercise of authority. The wife's power of being disagreeable generally only establishes a counter-tyranny, and makes victims in their turn chiefly of those husbands who are least inclined to be tyrants.

5. What is it, then, which really tempers the corrupting effects of the power, and makes it compatible with such amount of good as we actually see? Mere feminine blandishments, though of great effect in individual instances, have very little effect in modifying the general tendencies of the situation; for their power only lasts while the woman is young and attractive, often only while her charm is new, and not dimmed by familiarity; and on many men they have not much influence at any time. The real mitigating causes are, the personal affection which is the growth of time in so far as the man's nature is susceptible of it and the woman's character sufficiently congenial with his to excite it; their common interests as regards the children, and their general community of interest as concerns third persons (to which however there are very great limitations); the real importance of the wife to his daily comforts and enjoyments, and the value he consequently attaches to her on his personal account, which, in a man capable of feeling for others, lays the foundation of caring for her on her own; and lastly, the influence naturally acquired over almost all human beings by those near to their persons (if not actually disagree-

able to them): who, both by their direct entreaties, and by the insensible contagion of their feelings and dispositions, are often able, unless counteracted by some equally strong personal influence, to obtain a degree of command over the conduct of the superior, altogether excessive and unreasonable. Through these various means, the wife frequently exercises even too much power over the man; she is able to affect his conduct in things in which she may not be qualified to influence it for good—in which her influence may be not only unenlightened, but employed on the morally wrong side; and in which he would act better if left to his own prompting. But neither in the affairs of families nor in those of states is power a compensation for the loss of freedom. Her power often gives her what she has no right to, but does not enable her to assert her own rights. A Sultan's favourite slave has slaves under her, over whom she tyrannizes; but the desirable thing would be that she should neither have slaves nor be a slave. By entirely sinking her own existence in her husband; by having no will (or persuading him that she has no will) but his, in anything which regards their joint relation, and by making it the business of her life to work upon his sentiments, a wife may gratify herself by influencing, and very probably perverting, his conduct, in those of his external relations which she has never qualified herself to judge of, or in which she is herself wholly influenced by some personal or other partiality or prejudice. Accordingly, as things now are, those who act most kindly to their wives are quite as often made worse, as better, by the wife's influence, in respect to all interests extending beyond the family. She is taught that she has no business with things out of that sphere; and accordingly she seldom has any honest and conscientious opinion on them; and therefore hardly ever meddles with them for any legitimate purpose, but generally for an interested one. She neither knows nor cares which is the right side in politics, but she knows what will bring in money or invitations, give her husband a title, her son a place, or her daughter a good marriage.

6. But how, it will be asked, can any society exist without government? In a family, as in a state, some one person must be the ultimate ruler. Who shall decide when married people differ in opinion? Both cannot have their way, yet a decision one way or the other must be come to.

7. It is not true that in all voluntary association between two people, one of them must be absolute master: still less that the

law must determine which of them it shall be. The most frequent case of voluntary association, next to marriage, is partnership in business: and it is not found or thought necessary to enact that, in every partnership, one partner shall have entire control over the concern, and the others shall be bound to obey his orders. No one would enter into partnership on terms which would subject him to the responsibilities of a principal, with only the powers and privileges of a clerk or agent. If the law dealt with other contracts as it does with marriage, it would ordain that one partner should administer the common business as if it was his private concern; that the others should have only delegated powers; and that this one should be designated by some general presumption of law, for example as being the eldest. The law never does this: nor does experience show it to be necessary that any theoretical inequality of power should exist between the partners, or that the partnership should have any other conditions than what they may themselves appoint by their articles of agreement. Yet it might seem that the exclusive power might be conceded with less danger to the rights and interests of the inferior in the case of partnership than in that of marriage, since he is free to cancel the power by withdrawing from the connection. The wife has no such power, and even if she had, it is almost always desirable that she should try all measures before resorting to it.

8. It is quite true that things which have to be decided every day, and cannot adjust themselves gradually, or wait for a compromise, ought to depend on one will; one person must have their sole control. But it does not follow that this should always be the same person. The natural arrangement is a division of powers between the two; each being absolute in the executive branch of their own department, and any change of system and principle requiring the consent of both. The division neither can nor should be established by the law, since it must depend on individual capacities and suitabilities. If the two persons chose, they might pre-appoint it by the marriage contract, as pecuniary arrangements are now often pre-appointed. There would seldom be any difficulty in deciding such things by mutual consent, unless the marriage was one of those unhappy ones in which all other things, as well as this, become subjects of bickering and dispute. The division of rights would naturally follow the division of duties and functions; and that is already made by consent, or at all events not by law, but by general

custom, modified and modifiable at the pleasure of the persons
concerned.

9. The real practical decision of affairs, to whichever may be
given the legal authority, will greatly depend, as it even now
does, upon comparative qualifications. The mere fact that he is
usually the eldest will in most cases give the preponderance to
the man; at least until they both attain a time of life at which
the difference in their years is of no importance. There will
naturally also be a more potential voice on the side, whichever
it is, that brings the means of support. Inequality from this
source does not depend on the law of marriage, but on the
general conditions of human society, as now constituted. The
influence of mental superiority, either general or special, and of
superior decision of character, will necessarily tell for much. It
always does so at present. And this fact shows how little
foundation there is for the apprehension that the powers and
responsibilities of partners in life (as of partners in business)
cannot be satisfactorily apportioned by agreement between
themselves. They always are so apportioned, except in cases
in which the marriage institution is a failure. Things never
come to an issue of downright power on one side, and obedience
on the other, except where the connection altogether has been
a mistake, and it would be a blessing to both parties to be
relieved from it. Some may say that the very thing by which
an amicable settlement of differences becomes possible is the
power of legal compulsion known to be in reserve; as people
submit to an arbitration because there is a court of law in the
background, which they know that they can be forced to obey.
But to make the cases parallel, we must suppose that the rule
of the court of law was, not to try the cause, but to give judgment always for the same side, suppose the defendant. If so,
the amenability to it would be a motive with the plaintiff to
agree to almost any arbitration, but it would be just the reverse
with the defendant. The despotic power which the law gives
to the husband may be a reason to make the wife assent to
any compromise by which power is practically shared between the two, but it cannot be the reason why the husband
does. That there is always among decently conducted people
a practical compromise, though one of them at least is under no
physical or moral necessity of making it, shows that the natural
motives which lead to a voluntary adjustment of the united life
of two persons in a manner acceptable to both do, on the whole,

except in unfavourable cases, prevail. The matter is certainly not improved by laying down, as an ordinance of law, that the superstructure of free government shall be raised upon a legal basis of despotism on one side and subjection on the other, and that every concession which the despot makes may, at his mere pleasure, and without any warning, be recalled. Besides that no freedom is worth much when held on so precarious a tenure, its conditions are not likely to be the most equitable when the law throws so prodigious a weight into one scale; when the adjustment rests between two persons one of whom is declared to be entitled to everything, the other not only entitled to nothing except during the good pleasure of the first, but under the strongest moral and religious obligation not to rebel under any excess of oppression.

10. A pertinacious adversary, pushed to extremities, may say that husbands indeed are willing to be reasonable, and to make fair concessions to their partners, without being compelled to it, but that wives are not: that if allowed any rights of their own, they will acknowledge no rights at all in anyone else, and never will yield in anything, unless they can be compelled, by the man's mere authority, to yield in everything. This would have been said by many persons some generations ago, when satires on women were in vogue, and men thought it a clever thing to insult women for being what men made them. But it will be said by no one now who is worth replying to. It is not the doctrine of the present day that women are less susceptible of good feeling, and consideration for those with whom they are united by the strongest ties, than men are. On the contrary, we are perpetually told that women are better than men, by those who are totally opposed to treating them as if they were as good; so that the saying has passed into a piece of tiresome cant, intended to put a complimentary face upon an injury, and resembling those celebrations of royal clemency which, according to Gulliver, the king of Lilliput always prefixed to his most sanguinary decrees. If women are better than men in anything, it surely is in individual self-sacrifice for those of their own family. But I lay little stress on this, so long as they are universally taught that they are born and created for self-sacrifice. I believe that equality of rights would abate the exaggerated self-abnegation which is the present artificial ideal of feminine character, and that a good woman would not be more self-sacrificing than the best man: but, on the other hand,

men would be much more unselfish and self-sacrificing than at present, because they would no longer be taught to worship their own will as such a grand thing that it is actually the law for another rational being. There is nothing which men so easily learn as this self-worship : all privileged persons, and all privileged classes, have had it. The more we descend in the scale of humanity, the intenser it is; and most of all in those who are not, and can never expect to be, raised above anyone except an unfortunate wife and children. The honourable exceptions are proportionately fewer than in the case of almost any other human infirmity. Philosophy and religion, instead of keeping it in check, are generally suborned to defend it; and nothing controls it but that practical feeling of the equality of human beings which is the theory of Christianity, but which Christianity will never practically teach, while it sanctions institutions grounded on an arbitrary preference of one human being over another.

11. There are, no doubt, women, as there are men, whom equality of consideration will not satisfy; with whom there is no peace while any will or wish is regarded but their own. Such persons are a proper subject for the law of divorce. They are only fit to live alone, and no human beings ought to be compelled to associate their lives with them. But the legal subordination tends to make such characters among women more, rather than less, frequent. If the man exerts his whole power, the woman is of course crushed : but if she is treated with indulgence, and permitted to assume power, there is no rule to set limits to her encroachments. The law, not determining her rights, but theoretically allowing her none at all, practically declares that the measure of what she has a right to, is what she can contrive to get.

12. The equality of married persons before the law is not only the sole mode in which that particular relation can be made consistent with justice to both sides, and conducive to the happiness of both, but it is the only means of rendering the daily life of mankind, in any high sense, a school of moral cultivation. Though the truth may not be felt or generally acknowledged for generations to come, the only school of genuine moral sentiment is society between equals. The moral education of mankind has hitherto emanated chiefly from the law of force, and is adapted almost solely to the relations which force creates. In the less advanced states of society, people hardly

recognize any relation with their equals. To be an equal is to be an enemy. Society, from its highest place to its lowest, is one long chain, or rather ladder, where every individual is either above or below his nearest neighbour, and wherever he does not command he must obey. Existing moralities, accordingly, are mainly fitted to a relation of command and obedience. Yet command and obedience are but unfortunate necessities of human life; society in equality is its normal state. Already in modern life, and more and more as it progressively improves, command and obedience become exceptional facts in life, equal association its general rule. The morality of the first ages rested on the obligation to submit to power; that of the ages next following, on the right of the weak to the forbearance and protection of the strong. How much longer is one form of society and life to content itself with the morality made for another? We have had the morality of submission, and the morality of chivalry and generosity; the time is now come for the morality of justice. Whenever, in former ages, any approach has been made to society in equality, Justice has asserted its claim as the foundation of virtue. It was thus in the free republics of antiquity. But even in the best of these, the equals were limited to the free male citizens; slaves, women, and the unenfranchised residents were under the law of force. The joint influence of Roman civilization and of Christianity obliterated these distinctions, and in theory (if only partially in practice) declared the claims of the human being, as such, to be paramount to those of sex, class, or social position. The barriers which had begun to be levelled were raised again by the northern conquests; and the whole of modern history consists of the slow process by which they have since been wearing away. We are entering into an order of things in which justice will again be the primary virtue; grounded as before on equal, but now also on sympathetic association; having its root no longer in the instinct of equals for self-protection, but in a cultivated sympathy between them; and no one being now left out, but an equal measure being extended to all. It is no novelty that mankind do not distinctly foresee their own changes, and that their sentiments are adapted to past, not coming ages. To see the futurity of the species has always been the privilege of the intellectual élite or of those who have learnt from them; to have the feelings of that futurity has been the distinction, and usually the martyrdom, of a still rarer élite. Institutions, books, education, society, all go on training human beings for the old, long after the new has come; much more when it is only coming. But the true virtue of human beings is fitness to live together as equals; claiming nothing for themselves but what they as freely concede to every one else; regarding command of any kind as an exceptional necessity, and in all cases a temporary one ; and preferring, whenever possible, the society of those with whom leading and following can be alternate and reciprocal. To these virtues, nothing in life as at present constituted gives cultivation by exercise. The family is a school of despotism, in which the virtues of despotism, but also its vices, are largely nourished. Citizenship, in free countries, is partly a school of society in equality; but citizenship fills only a small place in modern life, and does not come near the daily habits or inmost sentiments. The family, justly constituted, would be the real school of the virtues of freedom. It is sure to be a sufficient one of everything else. It will always be a school of obedience for the children, of command for the parents. What is needed is, that it should be a school of sympathy in equality, of living together in love, without power on one side or obedience on the other. This it ought to be between the parents. It would then be an exercise of those virtues which each requires to fit them for all other association, and a model to the children of the feelings and conduct which their temporary training by means of obedience is designed to render habitual, and therefore natural, to them. The moral training of mankind will never be adapted to the conditions of the life for which all other human progress is a preparation, until they practise in the family the same moral rule which is adapted to the normal constitution of human society. Any sentiment of freedom which can exist in a man whose nearest and dearest intimacies are with those of whom he is absolute master, is not the genuine or Christian love of freedom, but, what the love of freedom generally was in the ancients and in the Middle Ages—an intense feeling of the dignity and importance of his own personality; making him disdain a yoke for himself, of which he has no abhorrence whatever in the abstract, but which he is abundantly ready to impose on others for his own interest or glorification.

13. I readily admit (and it is the very foundation of my hopes) that numbers of married people even under the present

law (in the higher classes of England probably a great majority)
live in the spirit of a just law of equality. Laws never would
be improved, if there were not numerous persons whose moral
sentiments are better than the existing laws. Such persons
ought to support the principles here advocated; of which the
only object is to make all other married couples similar to what
these are now. But persons even of considerable moral worth,
unless they are also thinkers, are very ready to believe that
laws or practices, the evils of which they have not personally
experienced, do not produce any evils, but (if seeming to be
generally approved of) probably do good, and that it is wrong
to object to them. It would, however, be a great mistake in
such married people to suppose, because the legal conditions
of the tie which unites them do not occur to their thoughts
once in a twelvemonth, and because they live and feel in all
respects as if they were legally equals, that the same is the
case with all other married couples, wherever the husband
is not a notorious ruffian. To suppose this, would be to show
equal ignorance of human nature and of fact. The less fit
a man is for the possession of power—the less likely to be
allowed to exercise it over any person with that person's
voluntary consent—the more does he hug himself in the consciousness of the power the law gives him, exact its legal rights
to the utmost point which custom (the custom of men like
himself) will tolerate, and take pleasure in using the power,
merely to enliven the agreeable sense of possessing it. What
is more; in the most naturally brutal and morally uneducated
part of the lower classes, the legal slavery of the woman, and
something in the merely physical subjection to their will as
an instrument, causes them to feel a sort of disrespect and
contempt towards their own wife which they do not feel towards
any other woman, or any other human being, with whom they
come in contact; and which makes her seem to them an appropriate subject for any kind of indignity. Let an acute observer
of the signs of feeling, who has the requisite opportunities,
judge for himself whether this is not the case: and if he finds
that it is, let him not wonder at any amount of disgust and
indignation that can be felt against institutions which lead
naturally to this depraved state of the human mind.

14. We shall be told, perhaps, that religion imposes the duty
of obedience; as every established fact which is too bad to
admit of any other defence is always presented to us as an

injunction of religion. The Church, it is very true, enjoins
it in her formularies, but it would be difficult to derive any such
injunction from Christianity. We are told that St. Paul said,
"Wives, obey your husbands"; but he also said, "Slaves, obey
your masters." It was not St. Paul's business, nor was it
consistent with his object, the propagation of Christianity, to
incite anyone to rebellion against existing laws. The Apostle's
acceptance of all social institutions as he found them, is no
more to be construed as a disapproval of attempts to improve
them at the proper time than his declaration, "The powers
that be are ordained of God," gives his sanction to military
despotism, and to that alone, as the Christian form of political
government, or commands passive obedience to it. To pretend
that Christianity was intended to stereotype existing forms
of government and society, and protect them against change, is
to reduce it to the level of Islamism or of Brahminism. It
is precisely because Christianity has not done this that it has
been the religion of the progressive portion of mankind, and
Islamism, Brahminism, &c., have been those of the stationary
portions; or rather (for there is no such thing as a really
stationary society) of the declining portions. There have been
abundance of people, in all ages of Christianity, who tried to
make it something of the same kind; to convert us into a sort
of Christian Mussulmans, with the Bible for a Koran, pro-
hibiting all improvement: and great has been their power, and
many have had to sacrifice their lives in resisting them. But
they have been resisted, and the resistance has made us what
we are, and will yet make us what we are to be.

15. After what has been said respecting the obligation of
obedience, it is almost superfluous to say anything concerning
the more special point included in the general one—a woman's
right to her own property; for I need not hope that this treatise
can make any impression upon those who need anything to con-
vince them that a woman's inheritance or gains ought to be as
much her own after marriage as before. The rule is simple:
whatever would be the husband's or wife's if they were not
married, should be under their exclusive control during marriage;
which need not interfere with the power to tie up property by
settlement, in order to preserve it for children Some people
are sentimentally shocked at the idea of a separate interest in
money matters, as inconsistent with the ideal fusion of two
lives into one. For my own part, I am one of the strongest

supporters of community of goods, when resulting from an entire unity of feeling in the owners, which makes all things common between them. But I have no relish for a community of goods resting on the doctrine that what is mine is yours, but what is yours is not mine; and I should prefer to decline entering into such a compact with anyone, though I were myself the person to profit by it.

16. This particular injustice and oppression to women, which is, to common apprehensions, more obvious than all the rest, admits of remedy without interfering with any other mischiefs: and there can be little doubt that it will be one of the earliest remedied. Already, in many of the new and several of the old States of the American Confederation, provisions have been inserted even in the written Constitutions, securing to women equality of rights in this respect; and thereby improving materially the position, in the marriage relation, of those women at least who have property, by leaving them one instrument of power which they have not signed away; and preventing also the scandalous abuse of the marriage institution, which is perpetrated when a man entraps a girl into marrying him without a settlement, for the sole purpose of getting possession of her money. When the support of the family depends, not on property, but on earnings, the common arrangement, by which the man earns the income and the wife superintends the domestic expenditure, seems to me in general the most suitable division of labour between the two persons. If, in addition to the physical suffering of bearing children, and the whole responsibility of their care and education in early years, the wife undertakes the careful and economical application of the husband's earnings to the general comfort of the family; she takes not only her fair share, but usually the larger share, of the bodily and mental exertion required by their joint existence. If she undertakes any additional portion, it seldom relieves her from this, but only prevents her from performing it properly. The care which she is herself disabled from taking of the children and the household, nobody else takes; those of the children who do not die grow up as they best can, and the management of the household is likely to be so bad as even in point of economy to be a great drawback from the value of the wife's earnings. In an otherwise just state of things, it is not, therefore, I think, a desirable custom that the wife should contribute by her labour to the income of the family. In an unjust

state of things, her doing so may be useful to her, by making
her of more value in the eyes of the man who is legally her
master; but, on the other hand, it enables him still farther to
abuse his power, by forcing her to work, and leaving the support
of the family to her exertions, while he spends most of his time
in drinking and idleness. The *power* of earning is essential to
the dignity of a woman, if she has not independent property.
But if marriage were an equal contract, not implying the obligation of obedience; if the connection were no longer enforced to
the oppression of those to whom it is purely a mischief, but
a separation, on just terms (I do not now speak of a divorce),
could be obtained by any woman who was morally entitled to it;
and if she would then find all honourable employments as freely
open to her as to men; it would not be necessary for her protection that during marriage she should make this particular
use of her faculties.   Like a man when he chooses a profession,
so, when a woman marries, it may in general be understood that
she makes choice of the management of a household, and the
bringing up of a family, as the first call upon her exertions,
during as many years of her life as may be required for the purpose; and that she renounces, not all other objects and occupations, but all which are not consistent with the requirements of
this.   The actual exercise, in a habitual or systematic manner,
of outdoor occupations, or such as cannot be carried on at home,
would by this principle be practically interdicted to the greater
number of married women.   But the utmost latitude ought to
exist for the adaptation of general rules to individual suitabilities; and there ought to be nothing to prevent faculties exceptionally adapted to any other pursuit from obeying their
vocation notwithstanding marriage: due provision being made
for supplying otherwise any falling-short which might become
inevitable, in her full performance of the ordinary functions of
mistress of a family.   These things, if once opinion were rightly
directed on the subject, might with perfect safety be left to be
regulated by opinion, without any interference of law.

CHAPTER III

1. On the other point which is involved in the just equality of women, their admissibility to all the functions and occupations hitherto retained as the monopoly of the stronger sex, I should anticipate no difficulty in convincing anyone who has gone with me on the subject of the equality of women in the family. I believe that their disabilities elsewhere are only clung to in order to maintain their subordination in domestic life; because the generality of the male sex cannot yet tolerate the idea of living with an equal. Were it not for that, I think that almost every one, in the existing state of opinion in politics and political economy, would admit the injustice of excluding half the human race from the greater number of lucrative occupations, and from almost all high social functions; ordaining from their birth either that they are not, and cannot by any possibility become, fit for employments which are legally open to the stupidest and basest of the other sex, or else that, however fit they may be, those employments shall be interdicted to them, in order to be preserved for the exclusive benefit of males. In the last two centuries, when (which was seldom the case) any reason beyond the mere existence of the fact was thought to be required to justify the disabilities of women, people seldom assigned as a reason their inferior mental capacity; which, in times when there was a real trial of personal faculties (from which all women were not excluded) in the struggles of public life, no one really believed in. The reason given in those days was not women's unfitness, but the interest of society, by which was meant the interest of men · just as the *raison d'état*, meaning the convenience of the government, and the support of existing authority, was deemed a sufficient explanation and excuse for the most flagitious crimes. In the present day, power holds a smoother language, and, whomsoever it oppresses, always pretends to do so for their own good: accordingly, when anything is forbidden to women, it is thought necessary to say, and

desirable to believe, that they are incapable of doing it, and that they depart from their real path of success and happiness when they aspire to it.   But to make this reason plausible (I do not say valid), those by whom it is urged must be prepared to carry it to a much greater length than anyone ventures to do in the face of present experience.   It is not sufficient to maintain that women on the average are less gifted than men on the average, with certain of the higher mental faculties, or that a smaller number of women than of men are fit for occupations and functions of the highest intellectual character.   It is necessary to maintain that no women at all are fit for them, and that the most eminent women are inferior in mental faculties to the most mediocre of the men on whom those functions at present devolve. For if the performance of the function is decided either by competition or by any mode of choice which secures regard to the public interest, there need be no apprehension that any important employments will fall into the hands of women inferior to average men, or to the average of their male competitors.   The only result would be that there would be fewer women than men in such employments; a result certain to happen in any case, if only from the preference always likely to be felt by the majority of women for the one vocation in which there is nobody to compete with them.   Now, the most determined depreciator of women will not venture to deny that, when we add the experience of recent times to that of ages past, women, and not a few merely, but many women, have proved themselves capable of everything, perhaps without a single exception, which is done by men, and of doing it successfully and creditably.   The utmost that can be said is, that there are many things which none of them have succeeded in doing as well as they have been done by some men—many in which they have not reached the very highest rank.   But there are extremely few, dependent only on mental faculties, in which they have not attained the rank next to the highest.   Is not this enough, and much more than enough, to make it a tyranny to them, and a detriment to society, that they should not be allowed to compete with men for the exercise of these functions ?   Is it not a mere truism to say, that such functions are often filled by men far less fit for them than numbers of women, and who would be beaten by women in any fair field of competition ?   What difference does it make that there may be men somewhere, fully employed about other things, who may be still better qualified for the things in question than these women ? Does not this take place in all competitions ? Is there so great a superfluity of men fit for high duties, that society can afford to reject the service of any competent person ? Are we so certain of always finding a man made to our hands for any duty or function of social importance which falls vacant, that we lose nothing by putting a ban upon one-half of mankind, and refusing beforehand to make their faculties available, however distinguished they may be? And even if we could do without them, would it be consistent with justice to refuse to them their fair share of honour and distinction, or to deny to them the equal moral right of all human beings to choose their occupation (short of injury to others) according to their own preferences, at their own risk? Nor is the injustice confined to them: it is shared by those who are in a position to benefit by their services. To ordain that any kind of persons shall not be physicians, or shall not be advocates, or shall not be members of parliament, is to injure not them only, but all who employ physicians or advocates, or elect members of parliament, and who are deprived of the stimulating effect of greater competition on the exertions of the competitors, as well as restricted to a narrower range of individual choice.

2. It will perhaps be sufficient if I confine myself, in the details of my argument, to functions of a public nature : since, if I am successful as to those, it probably will be readily granted that women should be admissible to all other occupations to which it is at all material whether they are admitted or not. And here let me begin by marking out one function, broadly distinguished from all others, their right to which is entirely independent of any question which can be raised concerning their faculties. I mean the suffrage, both parliamentary and municipal. The right to share in the choice of those who are to exercise a public trust is altogether a distinct thing from that of competing for the trust itself. If no one could vote for a member of parliament who was not fit to be a candidate, the government would be a narrow oligarchy indeed. To have a voice in choosing those by whom one is to be governed is a means of self-protection due to every one, though he were to remain for ever excluded from the function of governing; and that women are considered fit to have such a choice may be presumed, from the fact that the law already gives it to women in the most important of all cases to them-

selves: for the choice of the man who is to govern a woman to
the end of life is always supposed to be voluntarily made by
herself. In the case of election to public trusts, it is the
business of constitutional law to surround the right of suffrage
with all needful securities and limitations; but whatever
securities are sufficient in the case of the male sex, no others
need be required in the case of women. Under whatever
conditions, and within whatever limits, men are admitted to
the suffrage, there is not a shadow of justification for not
admitting women under the same. The majority of the
women of any class are not likely to differ in political opinion
from the majority of the men of the same class, unless the
question be one in which the interests of women, as such, are
in some way involved; and if they are so, women require the
suffrage, as their guarantee of just and equal consideration.
This ought to be obvious even to those who coincide in no
other of the doctrines for which I contend. Even if every
woman were a wife, and if every wife ought to be a slave, all
the more would these slaves stand in need of legal protection:
and we know what legal protection the slaves have, where the
laws are made by their masters.

3. With regard to the fitness of women, not only to participate in elections, but themselves to hold offices or practise
professions involving important public responsibilities; I have
already observed that this consideration is not essential to the
practical question in dispute: since any woman who succeeds
in an open profession proves by that very fact that she is
qualified for it. And in the case of public offices, if the
political system of the country is such as to exclude unfit men,
it will equally exclude unfit women: while if it is not, there is
no additional evil in the fact that the unfit persons whom it
admits may be either women or men. As long therefore as it
is acknowledged that even a few women may be fit for these
duties, the laws which shut the door on those exceptions
cannot be justified by any opinion which can be held respecting
the capacities of women in general. But, though this last consideration is not essential, it is far from being irrelevant. An
unprejudiced view of it gives additional strength to the arguments against the disabilities of women, and reinforces them
by high considerations of practical utility.

4. Let us at first make entire abstraction of all psychological
considerations tending to show that any of the mental differ-

ences supposed to exist between women and men are but the natural effect of the differences in their education and circumstances, and indicate no radical difference, far less radical inferiority, of nature. Let us consider women only as they already are, or as they are known to have been; and the capacities which they have already practically shown. What they have done, that at least, if nothing else, it is proved that they can do. When we consider how sedulously they are all trained away from, instead of being trained towards, any of the occupations or objects reserved for men, it is evident that I am taking a very humble ground for them, when I rest their case on what they have actually achieved. For, in this case, negative evidence is worth little, while any positive evidence is conclusive. It cannot be inferred to be impossible that a woman should be a Homer, or an Aristotle, or a Michael Angelo, or a Beethoven, because no woman has yet actually produced works comparable to theirs in any of those lines of excellence. This negative fact at most leaves the question uncertain, and open to psychological discussion. But it is quite certain that a woman can be a Queen Elizabeth, or a Deborah, or a Joan of Arc, since this is not inference, but fact. Now, it is a curious consideration that the only things which the existing law excludes women from doing are the things which they have proved that they are able to do. There is no law to prevent a woman from having written all the plays of Shakespeare, or composed all the operas of Mozart. But Queen Elizabeth or Queen Victoria, had they not inherited the throne, could not have been entrusted with the smallest of the political duties of which the former showed herself equal to the greatest.

5. If anything conclusive could be inferred from experience, without psychological analysis, it would be that the things which women are not allowed to do are the very ones for which they are peculiarly qualified; since their vocation for government has made its way, and become conspicuous, through the very few opportunities which have been given; while in the lines of distinction which apparently were freely open to them, they have by no means so eminently distinguished themselves. We know how small a number of reigning queens history presents, in comparison with that of kings. Of this smaller number a far larger proportion have shown talents for rule; though many of them have occupied the throne in difficult periods. It is

remarkable, too, that they have, in a great number of instances, been distinguished by merits the most opposite to the imaginary and conventional character of women : they have been as much remarked for the firmness and vigour of their rule as for its intelligence.   When to queens and empresses we add regents, and viceroys of provinces, the list of women who have been eminent rulers of mankind swells to a great length.[1]   This fact is so undeniable that some one, long ago, tried to retort the argument, and turned the admitted truth into an additional insult, by saying that queens are better than kings, because under kings women govern, but under queens men.

6. It may seem a waste of reasoning to argue against a bad joke; but such things do affect people's minds; and I have heard men quote this saying, with an air as if they thought that there was something in it. At any rate, it will serve as well as anything else for a starting-point in discussion. I say, then, that it is not true that under kings women govern. Such cases are entirely exceptional: and weak kings have quite as often governed ill through the influence of male favourites as of female. When a king is governed by a woman merely through his amatory propensities, good government is not probable, though even then there are exceptions. But French history counts two kings who have voluntarily given the direction of affairs during many years, the one to his mother, the other to his sister: one of them, Charles VIII., was a mere boy, but in doing so he followed the intentions of his father Louis XI., the ablest monarch of his age. The other, Saint Louis, was the best, and one of the most vigorous rulers, since the time of

---

[1] Especially is this true if we take into consideration Asia as well as Europe. If a Hindoo principality is strongly, vigilantly, and economically governed; if order is preserved without oppression; if cultivation is extending, and the people prosperous, in three cases out of four that principality is under a woman's rule. This fact, to me an entirely unexpected one, I have collected from a long official knowledge of Hindoo governments. There are many such instances: for though, by Hindoo institutions, a woman cannot reign, she is the legal regent of a kingdom during the minority of the heir; and minorities are frequent, the lives of the male rulers being so often prematurely terminated through the effect of inactivity and sensual excesses. When we consider that these princesses have never been seen in public, have never conversed with any man not of their own family except from behind a curtain, that they do not read, and, if they did, there is no book in their languages which can give them the smallest instruction on political affairs; the example they afford of the natural capacity of women for government is very striking.

Charlemagne. Both these princesses ruled in a manner hardly equalled by any prince among their contemporaries. The Emperor Charles the Fifth, the most politic prince of his time, who had as great a number of able men in his service as a ruler ever had, and was one of the least likely of all sovereigns to sacrifice his interest to personal feelings, made two princesses of his family successively Governors of the Netherlands, and kept one or other of them in that post during his whole life (they were afterwards succeeded by a third). Both ruled very successfully, and one of them, Margaret of Austria, was one of the ablest politicians of the age. So much for one side of the question. Now as to the other. When it is said that under queens men govern, is the same meaning to be understood as when kings are said to be governed by women? Is it meant that queens choose as their instruments of government the associates of their personal pleasures? The case is rare, even with those who are as unscrupulous on the latter point as Catherine II.: and it is not in these cases that the good government alleged to arise from male influence is to be found. If it be true, then, that the administration is in the hands of better men under a queen than under an average king, it must be that queens have a superior capacity for choosing them; and women must be better qualified than men both for the position of sovereign, and for that of chief minister; for the principal business of a prime minister is not to govern in person, but to find the fittest persons to conduct every department of public affairs. The more rapid insight into character, which is one of the admitted points of superiority in women over men, must certainly make them, with anything like parity of qualifications in other respects, more apt than men in that choice of instruments which is nearly the most important business of every one who has to do with governing mankind. Even the unprincipled Catherine de' Medici could feel the value of a Chancellor de l'Hôpital. But it is also true that most great queens have been great by their own talents for government, and have been well served precisely for that reason. They retained the supreme direction of affairs in their own hands: and if they listened to good advisers, they gave by that fact the strongest proof that their judgment fitted them for dealing with the great questions of government.

7. Is it reasonable to think that those who are fit for the greater functions of politics, are incapable of qualifying them-

selves for the less! Is there any reason in the nature of things
that the wives and sisters of princes should, whenever called on,
be found as competent as the princes themselves to *their* business,
but that the wives and sisters of statesmen, and administrators,
and directors of companies, and managers of public institutions,
should be unable to do what is done by their brothers and
husbands? The real reason is plain enough; it is that
princesses, being more raised above the generality of men
by their rank than placed below them by their sex, have never
been taught that it was improper for them to concern themselves
with politics; but have been allowed to feel the liberal interest
natural to any cultivated human being in the great transactions which took place around them, and in which they might
be called on to take a part. The ladies of reigning families are
the only women who are allowed the same range of interests
and freedom of development as men; and it is precisely in
their case that there is not found to be any inferiority.
Exactly where and in proportion as women's capacities for
government have been tried, in that proportion have they been
found adequate.

8. This fact is in accordance with the best general conclusions
which the world's imperfect experience seems as yet to suggest,
concerning the peculiar tendencies and aptitudes characteristic of women, as women have hitherto been. I do not say, as
they will continue to be; for, as I have already said more than
once, I consider it presumption in anyone to pretend to decide
what women are or are not, can or cannot be, by natural
constitution. They have always hitherto been kept, as far as
regards spontaneous development, in so unnatural a state that
their nature cannot but have been greatly distorted and dis-
guised: and no one can safely pronounce that if women's
nature were left to choose its direction as freely as men's, and if
no artificial bent were attempted to be given to it except that
required by the conditions of human society, and given to
both sexes alike, there would be any material difference, or
perhaps any difference at all, in the character and capacities
which would unfold themselves. I shall presently show, that
even the least contestable of the differences which now exist
are such as may very well have been produced merely by
circumstances, without any difference of natural capacity. But,
looking at women as they are known in experience, it may
be said of them, with more truth than belongs to most other

generalizations on the subject, that the general bent of their talents is toward the practical. This statement is conformable to all the public history of women, in the present and the past. It is no less borne out by common and daily experience. Let us consider the special nature of the mental capacities most characteristic of a woman of talent. They are all of a kind which fits them for practice, and makes them tend towards it. What is meant by a woman's capacity of intuitive perception? It means, a rapid and correct insight into present fact. It has nothing to do with general principles. Nobody ever perceived a scientific law of nature by intuition, nor arrived at a general rule of duty or prudence by it. These are results of slow and careful collection and comparison of experience; and neither the men nor the women of intuition usually shine in this department, unless, indeed, the experience necessary is such as they can acquire by themselves. For what is called their intuitive sagacity makes them peculiarly apt in gathering such general truths as can be collected from their individual means of observation. When, consequently, they chance to be as well provided as men are with the results of other people's experience, by reading and education (I use the word chance advisedly, for, in respect to the knowledge that tends to fit them for the greater concerns of life, the only educated women are the self-educated), they are better furnished than men in general with the essential requisites of skilful and successful practice. Men who have been much taught are apt to be deficient in the sense of present fact; they do not see, in the facts which they are called upon to deal with, what is really there, but what they have been taught to expect. This is seldom the case with women of any ability. Their capacity of "intuition" preserves them from it. With equality of experience and of general faculties, a woman usually sees much more than a man of what is immediately before her. Now, this sensibility to the present is the main quality on which the capacity for practice, as distinguished from theory, depends. To discover general principles belongs to the speculative faculty: to discern and discriminate the particular cases in which they are and are not applicable constitutes practical talent: and for this, women as they now are have a peculiar aptitude. I admit that there can be no good practice without principles, and that the predominant place which quickness of observation holds among a woman's faculties makes her particularly apt to build overhasty generalizations upon her own observation; though at the same time no less ready in rectifying those generalizations, as her observation takes a wider range. But the corrective to this defect is access to the experience of the human race; general knowledge—exactly the thing which education can best supply. A woman's mistakes are specifically those of a clever self-educated man, who often sees what men trained in routine do not see, but falls into errors for want of knowing things which have long been known. Of course he has acquired much of the pre-existing knowledge, or he could not have got on at all; but what he knows of it he has picked up in fragments and at random, as women do.

9. But this gravitation of women's minds to the present, to the real, to actual fact, while in its exclusiveness it is a source of errors, is also a most useful counteractive of the contrary error. The principal and most characteristic aberration of speculative minds, as such, consists precisely in the deficiency of this lively perception and ever-present sense of objective fact. For want of this, they often not only overlook the contradiction which outward facts oppose to their theories, but lose sight of the legitimate purpose of speculation altogether, and let their speculative faculties go astray into regions not peopled with real beings, animate or inanimate, even idealized, but with personified shadows created by the illusions of metaphysics or by the mere entanglement of words, and think these shadows the proper objects of the highest, the most transcendent, philosophy. Hardly anything can be of greater value to a man of theory and speculation who employs himself, not in collecting materials of knowledge by observation, but in working them up by processes of thought into comprehensive truths of science and laws of conduct, than to carry on his speculations in the companionship, and under the criticism, of a really superior woman. There, is nothing comparable to it for keeping his thoughts within the limits of real things, and the actual facts of nature. A woman seldom runs wild after an abstraction. The habitual direction of her mind to dealing with things as individuals rather than in groups, and (what is closely connected with it) her more lively interest in the present feelings of persons, which makes her consider first of all, in anything which claims to be applied to practice, in what manner persons will be affected by it—these two things make her extremely unlikely to put faith in any speculation which loses sight of

individuals, and deals with things as if they existed for the benefit of some imaginary entity, some mere creation of the mind, not resolvable into the feelings of living beings. Women's thoughts are thus as useful in giving reality to those of thinking men, as men's thoughts in giving width and largeness to those of women. In depth, as distinguished from breadth, I greatly doubt if even now women, compared with men, are at any disadvantage.

10. If the existing mental characteristics of women are thus valuable even in aid of speculation, they are still more important, when speculation has done its work, for carrying out the results of speculation into practice. For the reasons already given, women are comparatively unlikely to fall into the common error of men, that of sticking to their rules in a case whose specialities either take it out of the class to which the rules are applicable, or require a special adaptation of them. Let us now consider another of the admitted superiorities of clever women, greater quickness of apprehension. Is not this pre-eminently a quality which fits a person for practice? In action, everything continually depends upon deciding promptly. In speculation, nothing does. A mere thinker can wait, can take time to consider, can collect additional evidence; he is not obliged to complete his philosophy at once, lest the opportunity should go by. The power of drawing the best conclusion possible from insufficient data is not indeed useless in philosophy; the construction of a provisional hypothesis consistent with all known facts is often the needful basis for further inquiry. But this faculty is rather serviceable in philosophy than the main qualification for it: and, for the auxiliary as well as for the main operation, the philosopher can allow himself any time he pleases. He is in no need of the capacity of doing rapidly what he does; what he rather needs is patience, to work on slowly until imperfect lights have become perfect, and a conjecture has ripened into a theorem. For those, on the contrary, whose business is with the fugitive and perishable—with individual facts, not kinds of facts—rapidity of thought is a qualification next only in importance to the power of thought itself. He who has not his faculties under immediate command, in the contingencies of action, might as well not have them at all. He may be fit to criticize, but he is not fit to act. Now, it is in this that women, and the men who are most like women, confessedly excel. The other sort of man, however pre-eminent

may be his faculties, arrives slowly at complete command of them: rapidity of judgment and promptitude of judicious action, even in the things he knows best, are the gradual and late result of strenuous effort grown into habit.

11. It will be said, perhaps, that the greater nervous susceptibility of women is a disqualification for practice, in anything but domestic life, by rendering them mobile, changeable, too vehemently under the influence of the moment, incapable of dogged perseverance, unequal and uncertain in the power of using their faculties. I think that these phrases sum up the greater part of the objections commonly made to the fitness of women for the higher class of serious business. Much of all this is the mere overflow of nervous energy run to waste, and would cease when the energy was directed to a definite end. Much is also the result of conscious or unconscious cultivation; as we see by the almost total disappearance of "hysterics" and fainting-fits, since they have gone out of fashion. Moreover, when people are brought up, like many women of the higher classes (though less so in our own country than in any other), a kind of hothouse plants, shielded from the wholesome vicissitudes of air and temperature, and untrained in any of the occupations and exercises which give stimulus and development to the circulatory and muscular system, while their nervous system, especially in its emotional department, is kept in unnaturally active play; it is no wonder if those of them who do not die of consumption, grow up with constitutions liable to derangement from slight causes, both internal and external, and without stamina to support any task, physical or mental, requiring continuity of effort. But women brought up to work for their livelihood show none of these morbid characteristics, unless indeed they are chained to an excess of sedentary work in confined and unhealthy rooms. Women who in their early years have shared in the healthful physical education and bodily freedom of their brothers, and who obtain a sufficiency of pure air and exercise in after-life, very rarely have any excessive susceptibility of nerves which can disqualify them for active pursuits. There is indeed a certain proportion of persons, in both sexes, in whom an unusual degree of nervous sensibility is constitutional, and of so marked a character as to be the feature of their organization which exercises the greatest influence over the whole character of the vital phenomena. This constitution, like other physical conformations, is hereditary, and is trans-

mitted to sons as well as daughters; but it is possible, and probable, that the nervous temperament (as it is called) is inherited by a greater number of women than of men. We will assume this as a fact: and let me then ask, are men of nervous temperament found to be unfit for the duties and pursuits usually followed by men? If not, why should women of the same temperament be unfit for them? The peculiarities of the temperament are, no doubt, within certain limits, an obstacle to success in some employments, though an aid to it in others. But when the occupation is suitable to the temperament, and sometimes even when it is unsuitable, the most brilliant examples of success are continually given by the men of high nervous sensibility. They are distinguished in their practical manifestations chiefly by this, that, being susceptible of a higher degree of excitement than those of another physical constitution, their powers when excited differ more than in the case of other people from those shown in their ordinary state: they are raised, as it were, above themselves, and do things with ease which they are wholly incapable of at other times. But this lofty excitement is not, except in weak bodily constitutions, a mere flash, which passes away immediately, leaving no permanent traces, and incompatible with persistent and steady pursuit of an object. It is the character of the nervous temperament to be capable of *sustained* excitement, holding out through long-continued efforts. It is what is meant by *spirit*. It is what makes the high-bred racehorse run without slackening speed till he drops down dead. It is what has enabled so many delicate women to maintain the most sublime constancy not only at the stake, but through a long preliminary succession of mental and bodily tortures. It is evident that people of this temperament are particularly apt for what may be called the executive department of the leadership of mankind. They are the material of great orators, great preachers, impressive diffusers of moral influences. Their constitution might be deemed less favourable to the qualities required from a statesman in the cabinet, or from a judge. It would be so, if the consequence necessarily followed that because people are excitable they must always be in a state of excitement. But this is wholly a question of training. Strong feeling is the instrument and element of strong self-control: but it requires to be cultivated in that direction. When it is, it forms not the heroes of impulse only, but those also of self-conquest. History

and experience prove that the most passionate characters are
the most frantically rigid in their feelings of duty, when their
passion has been trained to act in that direction. The judge
who gives a just decision in a case where his feelings are intensely interested on the other side, derives from that same
strength of feeling the determined sense of the obligation of
justice, which enables him to achieve this victory over himself.
The capability of that lofty enthusiasm which takes the human
being out of his everyday character reacts upon the daily
character itself. His aspirations and powers when he is in this
exceptional state become the type with which he compares,
and by which he estimates, his sentiments and proceedings at
other times: and his habitual purposes assume a character
moulded by and assimilated to the moments of lofty excitement,
although those, from the physical nature of a human being, can
only be transient. Experience of races, as well as of individuals,
does not show those of excitable temperament to be less fit, on
the average, either for speculation or practice, than the most
unexcitable. The French, and the Italians, are undoubtedly by
nature more nervously excitable than the Teutonic races, and,
compared at least with the English, they have a much greater
habitual and daily emotional life : but have they been less great
in science, in public business, in legal and judicial eminence, or
in war ? There is abundant evidence that the Greeks were of
old, as their descendants and successors still are, one of the more
excitable of the races of mankind. It is superfluous to ask what,
among the achievements of men, they did not excel in. The
Romans, probably, as an equally southern people, had the same
original temperament : but the stern character of their national
discipline, like that of the Spartans, made them an example of
the opposite type of national character; the greater strength of
their natural feelings being chiefly apparent in the intensity
which the same original temperament made it possible to give
to the artificial. If these cases exemplify what a naturally
excitable people may be made, the Irish Celts afford one of the
aptest examples of what they are when left to themselves; (if
those can be said to be left to themselves who have been for
centuries under the indirect influence of bad government, and
the direct training of a Catholic hierarchy and of a sincere belief
in the Catholic religion). The Irish character must be considered, therefore, as an unfavourable case : yet, whenever the
circumstances of the individual have been at all favourable, what

people have shown greater capacity for the most varied and multifarious individual eminence? Like the French compared with the English, the Irish with the Swiss, the Greeks or Italians compared with the German races, so women compared with men may be found, on the average, to do the same things, with some variety in the particular kind of excellence. But that they would do them fully as well on the whole, if their education and cultivation were adapted to correcting instead of aggravating the infirmities incident to their temperament, I see not the smallest reason to doubt.

12. Supposing it, however, to be true that women's minds are by nature more mobile than those of men, less capable of persisting long in the same continuous effort, more fitted for dividing their faculties among many things than for travelling in any one path to the highest point which can be reached by it: this may be true of women as they now are (though not without great and numerous exceptions), and may account for their having remained behind the highest order of men in precisely the things in which this absorption of the whole mind in one set of ideas and occupations may seem to be most requisite. Still, this difference is one which can only affect the kind of excellence, not the excellence itself, or its practical worth: and it remains to be shown whether this exclusive working of a part of the mind, this absorption of the whole thinking faculty in a single subject, and concentration of it on a single work, is the normal and healthful condition of the human faculties, even for speculative uses. I believe that what is gained in special development by this concentration, is lost in the capacity of the mind for the other purposes of life; and, even in abstract thought, it is my decided opinion that the mind does more by frequently returning to a difficult problem, than by sticking to it without interruption. For the purposes, at all events, of practice, from its highest to its humblest departments, the capacity of passing promptly from one subject of consideration to another, without letting the active spring of the intellect run down between the two, is a power far more valuable; and this power women pre-eminently possess, by virtue of the very mobility of which they are accused. They perhaps have it from nature, but they certainly have it by training and education; for nearly the whole of the occupations of women consist in the management of small but multitudinous details, on each of which the mind cannot dwell even for a minute, but must

pass on to other things, and if anything requires longer thought, must steal time at odd moments for thinking of it. The capacity indeed which women show for doing their thinking in circumstances and at times which almost any man would make an excuse to himself for not attempting it, has often been noticed: and a woman's mind, though it may be occupied only with small things, can hardly ever permit itself to be vacant, as a man's so often is when not engaged in what he chooses to consider the business of his life. The business of a woman's ordinary life is things in general, and can as little cease to go on as the world to go round.

13. But (it is said) there is anatomical evidence of the superior mental capacity of men compared with women: they have a larger brain. I reply, that in the first place the fact itself is doubtful. It is by no means established that the brain of a woman is smaller than that of a man. If it is inferred merely because a woman's bodily frame generally is of less dimensions than a man's, this criterion would lead to strange consequences. A tall and large-boned man must on this showing be wonderfully superior in intelligence to a small man, and an elephant or a whale must prodigiously excel mankind. The size of the brain in human beings, anatomists say, varies much less than the size of the body, or even of the head, and the one cannot be at all inferred from the other. It is certain that some women have as large a brain as any man. It is within my knowledge that a man who had weighed many human brains, said that the heaviest he knew of, heavier even than Cuvier's (the heaviest previously recorded), was that of a woman. Next, I must observe that the precise relation which exists between the brain and the intellectual powers is not yet well understood, but is a subject of great dispute. That there is a very close relation we cannot doubt. The brain is certainly the material organ of thought and feeling: and (making abstraction of the great unsettled controversy respecting the appropriation of different parts of the brain to different mental faculties) I admit that it would be an anomaly, and an exception to all we know of the general laws of life and organization, if the size of the organ were wholly indifferent to the function; if no accession of power were derived from the greater magnitude of the instrument. But the exception and the anomaly would be fully as great if the organ exercised influence by its magnitude *only*. In all the more delicate operations of nature—of which those of the ani-

mated creation are the most delicate, and those of the nervous
system by far the most delicate of these—differences in the
effect depend as much on differences of quality in the physical
agents as on their quantity : and if the quality of an instrument
is to be tested by the nicety and delicacy of the work it can do,
the indications point to a greater average fineness of quality in
the brain and nervous system of women than of men. Dis-
missing abstract difference of quality, a thing difficult to verify,
the efficiency of an organ is known to depend not solely on its
size but on its activity : and of this we have an approximate
measure in the energy with which the blood circulates through
it, both the stimulus and the reparative force being mainly dependent on the circulation. It would not be surprising—it is
indeed an hypothesis which accords well with the differences
actually observed between the mental operations of the two
sexes—if men on the average should have the advantage in the
size of the brain, and women in activity of cerebral circulation.
The results which conjecture, founded on analogy, would lead us
to expect from this difference of organization, would correspond
to some of those which we most commonly see. In the first
place, the mental operations of men might be expected to be
slower. They would neither be so prompt as women in thinking,
nor so quick to feel. Large bodies take more time to get into
full action. On the other hand, when once got thoroughly into
play, men's brain would bear more work. It would be more
persistent in the line first taken ; it would have more difficulty
in changing from one mode of action to another, but, in the one
thing it was doing, it could go on longer without loss of power
or sense of fatigue. And do we not find that the things in
which men most excel women are those which require most
plodding and long hammering at a single thought, while women
do best what must be done rapidly ? A woman's brain is sooner
fatigued, sooner exhausted ; but, given the degree of exhaustion,
we should expect to find that it would recover itself sooner.
I repeat that this speculation is entirely hypothetical ; it pretends to no more than to suggest a line of inquiry. I have
before repudiated the notion of its being yet certainly known
that there is any natural difference at all in the average strength
or direction of the mental capacities of the two sexes, much less
what that difference is. Nor is it possible that this should be
known, so long as the psychological laws of the formation of
character have been so little studied, even in a general way, and

in the particular case never scientifically applied at all; so long
as the most obvious external causes of difference of character are
habitually disregarded—left unnoticed by the observer, and
looked down upon with a kind of supercilious contempt by the
prevalent schools both of natural history and of mental philosophy : who, whether they look for the source of what mainly
distinguishes human beings from one another in the world of
matter or in that of spirit, agree in running down those who
prefer to explain these differences by the different relations of
human beings to society and life.

14. To so ridiculous an extent are the notions formed of the
nature of women mere empirical generalizations, framed, without philosophy or analysis, upon the first instances which present
themselves, that the popular idea of it is different in different
countries, according as the opinions and social circumstances of
the country have given to the women living in it any speciality
of development or non-development. An Oriental thinks that
women are by nature peculiarly voluptuous; see the violent
abuse of them on this ground in Hindoo writings. An Englishman usually thinks that they are by nature cold. The sayings
about women's fickleness are mostly of French origin; from the
famous distich of Francis the First, upward and downward. In
England it is a common remark how much more constant
women are than men. Inconstancy has been longer reckoned
discreditable to a woman in England than in France; and
Englishwomen are besides, in their inmost nature, much more
subdued to opinion. It may be remarked by the way, that
Englishmen are in peculiarly unfavourable circumstances for
attempting to judge what is or is not natural, not merely to
women, but to men, or to human beings altogether, at least if
they have only English experience to go upon: because there
is no place where human nature shows so little of its original
lineaments. Both in a good and a bad sense, the English are
farther from a state of nature than any other modern people.
They are, more than any other people, a product of civilization
and discipline. England is the country in which social discipline has most succeeded, not so much in conquering as in
suppressing whatever is liable to conflict with it. The English,
more than any other people, not only act but feel according to
rule. In other countries, the taught opinion, or the requirement
of society, may be the stronger power, but the promptings of
the individual nature are always visible under it, and often re-

sisting it : rule may be stronger than nature, but nature is still there. In England, rule has to a great degree substituted itself for nature. The greater part of life is carried on, not by following inclination under the control of rule, but by having no inclination but that of following a rule. Now, this has its good side doubtless, though it has also a wretchedly bad one ; but it must render an Englishman peculiarly ill qualified to pass a judgment on the original tendencies of human nature from his own experience. The errors to which observers elsewhere are liable on the subject are of a different character. An Englishman is ignorant respecting human nature ; a Frenchman is prejudiced. An Englishman's errors are negative ; a Frenchman's positive. An Englishman fancies that things do not exist, because he never sees them ; a Frenchman thinks they must always and necessarily exist, because he does see them. An Englishman does not know nature, because he has had no opportunity of observing it ; a Frenchman generally knows a great deal of it, but often mistakes it, because he has only seen it sophisticated and distorted. For the artificial state superinduced by society disguises the natural tendencies of the thing which is the subject of observation, in two different ways ; by extinguishing the nature, or by transforming it. In the one case there is but a starved residuum of nature remaining to be studied ; in the other case there is much, but it may have expanded in any direction rather than that in which it would spontaneously grow.

15. I have said that it cannot now be known how much of the existing mental differences between men and women is natural, and how much artificial ; whether there are any natural differences at all ; or, supposing all artificial causes of difference to be withdrawn, what natural character would be revealed. I am not about to attempt what I have pronounced impossible : but doubt does not forbid conjecture, and, where certainty is unattainable, there may yet be the means of arriving at some degree of probability. The first point, the origin of the differences actually observed, is the one most accessible to speculation ; and I shall attempt to approach it by the only path by which it can be reached—by tracing the mental consequences of external influences. We cannot isolate a human being from the circumstances of his condition, so as to ascertain experimentally what he would have been by nature ; but we can consider what he is, and what his circumstances have been,

and whether the one would have been capable of producing the other.

16. Let us take, then, the only marked case which observation affords of apparent inferiority of women to men, if we except the merely physical one of bodily strength. No production in philosophy, science, or art, entitled to the first rank, has been the work of a woman. Is there any mode of accounting for this, without supposing that women are naturally incapable of producing them?

17. In the first place, we may fairly question whether experience has afforded sufficient grounds for an induction. It is scarcely three generations since women, saving very rare exceptions, have begun to try their capacity in philosophy, science, or art. It is only in the present generation that their attempts have been at all numerous; and they are even now extremely few, everywhere but in England and France. It is a relevant question, whether a mind possessing the requisites of first-rate eminence in speculation or creative art could have been expected, on the mere calculation of chances, to turn up, during that lapse of time, among the women whose tastes and personal position admitted of their devoting themselves to these pursuits. In all things which there has yet been time for—in all but the very highest grades in the scale of excellence, especially in the department in which they have been longest engaged, literature (both prose and poetry)—women have done quite as much, have obtained fully as high prizes and as many of them, as could be expected from the length of time and the number of competitors. If we go back to the earlier period when very few women made the attempt, yet some of those few made it with distinguished success. The Greeks always accounted Sappho among their great poets; and we may well suppose that Myrtis, said to have been the teacher of Pindar, and Corinna, who five times bore away from him the prize of poetry, must at least have had sufficient merit to admit of being compared with that great name. Aspasia did not leave any philosophical writings; but it is an admitted fact that Socrates resorted to her for instruction, and avowed himself to have obtained it.

18. If we consider the works of women in modern times, and contrast them with those of men, either in the literary or the artistic department, such inferiority as may be observed resolves itself essentially into one thing: but that is a most material one—deficiency of originality. Not total deficiency; for every

production of mind which is of any substantive value has an originality of its own—is a conception of the mind itself, not a copy of something else. Thoughts original, in the sense of being unborrowed—of being derived from the thinker's own observations or intellectual processes—are abundant in the writings of women. But they have not yet produced any of those great and luminous new ideas which form an era in thought, nor those fundamentally new conceptions in art which open a vista of possible effects not before thought of, and found a new school. Their compositions are mostly grounded on the existing fund of thought, and their creations do not deviate widely from existing types. This is the sort of inferiority which their works manifest: for in point of execution, in the detailed application of thought, and the perfection of style, there is no inferiority. Our best novelists, in point of composition and of the management of detail, have mostly been women ; and there is not in all modern literature a more eloquent vehicle of thought than the style of Madame de Staël, nor, as a specimen of purely artistic excellence, anything superior to the prose of Madame Sand, whose style acts upon the nervous system like a symphony of Haydn or Mozart. High originality of conception is, as I have said, what is chiefly wanting. And now to examine if there is any manner in which this deficiency can be accounted for.

19. Let us remember, then, so far as regards mere thought, that during all that period in the world's existence, and in the progress of cultivation, in which great and fruitful new truths could be arrived at by mere force of genius, with little previous study and accumulation of knowledge—during all that time women did not concern themselves with speculation at all. From the days of Hypatia to those of the Reformation, the illustrious Heloisa is almost the only woman to whom any such achievement might have been possible ; and we know not how great a capacity of speculation in her may have been lost to mankind by the misfortunes of her life. Never since any considerable number of women have begun to cultivate serious thought has originality been possible on easy terms. Nearly all the thoughts which can be reached by mere strength of original faculties have long since been arrived at ; and originality, in any high sense of the word, is now scarcely ever attained but by minds which, have undergone elaborate discipline, and are deeply versed in the results of previous thinking. It is Mr. Maurice,

I think, who has remarked on the present age, that its most original thinkers are those who have known most thoroughly what had been thought by their predecessors: and this will always henceforth be the case. Every fresh stone in the edifice has now to be placed on the top of so many others, that a long process of climbing, and of carrying up materials, has to be gone through by whoever aspires to take a share in the present stage of the work. How many women are there who have gone through any such process? Mrs. Somerville, alone perhaps of women, knows as much of mathematics as is now needful for making any considerable mathematical discovery: is it any proof of inferiority in women, that she has not happened to be one of the two or three persons who in her lifetime have associated their names with some striking advancement of the science? Two women, since political economy has been made a science, have known enough of it to write usefully on the subject: of how many of the innumerable men who have written on it during the same time is it possible with truth to say more? If no woman has hitherto been a great historian, what woman has had the necessary erudition? If no woman is a great philologist, what woman has studied Sanscrit and Slavonic, the Gothic of Ulphila and the Persic of the Zendavesta? Even in practical matters we all know what is the value of the originality of untaught geniuses. It means, inventing over again in its rudimentary form something already invented and improved upon by many successive inventors. When women have had the preparation which all men now require to be eminently original, it will be time enough to begin judging by experience of their capacity for originality.

20. It no doubt often happens that a person, who has not widely and accurately studied the thoughts of others on a subject, has by natural sagacity a happy intuition, which he can suggest, but cannot prove, which yet when matured may be an important addition to knowledge: but even then, no justice can be done to it until some other person, who does possess the previous acquirements, takes it in hand, tests it, gives it a scientific or practical form, and fits it into its place among the existing truths of philosophy or science. Is it supposed that such felicitous thoughts do not occur to women? They occur by hundreds to every woman of intellect. But they are mostly lost, for want of a husband or friend who has the other knowledge which can enable him to estimate them properly and

bring them before the world : and even when they are brought before it, they generally appear as his ideas, not their real author's. Who can tell how many of the most original thoughts put forth by male writers belong to a woman by suggestion, to themselves only by verifying and working out? If I may judge by my own case, a very large proportion indeed.

21. If we turn from pure speculation to literature in the narrow sense of the term, and the fine arts, there is a very obvious reason why women's literature is, in its general conception and in its main features, an imitation of men's. Why is the Roman literature, as critics proclaim to satiety, not original, but an imitation of the Greek? Simply because the Greeks came first. If women lived in a different country from men, and had never read any of their writings, they would have had a literature of their own. As it is, they have not created one, because they found a highly advanced literature already created. If there had been no suspension of the knowledge of antiquity, or if the Renaissance had occurred before the Gothic cathedrals were built, they never would have been built. We see that, in France and Italy, imitation of the ancient literature stopped the original development even after it had commenced. All women who write are pupils of the great male writers. A painter's early pictures, even if he be a Raffaelle, are undistinguishable in style from those of his master. Even a Mozart does not display his powerful originality in his earliest pieces. What years are to a gifted individual, generations are to a mass. If women's literature is destined to have a different collective character from that of men, depending on any difference of natural tendencies, much longer time is necessary than has yet elapsed before it can emancipate itself from the influence of accepted models, and guide itself by its own impulses. But if, as I believe, there will not prove to be any natural tendencies common to women, and distinguishing their genius from that of men, yet every individual writer among them has her individual tendencies, which at present are still subdued by the influence of precedent and example : and it will require generations more, before their individuality is sufficiently developed to make head against that influence.

22. It is in the fine arts, properly so called, that the primâ facie evidence of inferior original powers in women at first sight appears the strongest : since opinion (it may be said) does not

exclude them from these, but rather encourages them; and their education, instead of passing over this department, is in the affluent classes mainly composed of it. Yet in this line of exertion they have fallen still more short than in many others, of the highest eminence attained by men. This shortcoming, however, needs no other explanation than the familiar fact, more universally true in the fine arts than in anything else— the vast superiority of professional persons over amateurs. Women in the educated classes are almost universally taught more or less of some branch or other of the fine arts, but not that they may gain their living or their social consequence by it. Women artists are all amateurs. The exceptions are only of the kind which confirm the general truth. Women are taught music, but not for the purpose of composing, only of executing it: and accordingly it is only as composers that men, in music, are superior to women. The only one of the fine arts which women do follow, to any extent, as a profession, and an occupation for life, is the histrionic; and in that they are confessedly equal, if not superior, to men. To make the comparison fair, it should be made between the productions of women, in any branch of art, and those of men not following it as a profession. In musical composition, for example, women surely have produced fully as good things as have ever been produced by male amateurs. There are now a few women, a very few, who practise painting as a profession, and these are already beginning to show quite as much talent as could be expected. Even male painters (*pace* Mr. Ruskin) have not made any very remarkable figure these last centuries, and it will be long before they do so. The reason why the old painters were so greatly superior to the modern, is that a greatly superior class of men applied themselves to the art. In the fourteenth and fifteenth centuries the Italian painters were the most accomplished men of their age. The greatest of them were men of encyclopædical acquirements and powers, like the great men of Greece. But in their times fine art was, to men's feelings and conceptions, among the grandest things in which a human being could excel; and by it men were made, what only political or military distinction now makes them, the companions of sovereigns, and the equals of the highest nobility. In the present age, men of anything like similar calibre find something more important to do, for their own fame and the uses of the modern world, than painting: and it is only now and then that a Reynolds or a Turner (of whose relative rank among eminent men I do not pretend to an opinion) applies himself to that art. Music belongs to a different order of things; it does not require the same general powers of mind, but seems more dependent on a natural gift: and it may be thought surprising that no one of the great musical composers has been a woman. But even this natural gift, to be made available for great creations, requires study, and professional devotion to the pursuit. The only countries which have produced first-rate composers, even of the male sex, are Germany and Italy—countries in which, both in point of special and of general cultivation, women have remained far behind France and England, being generally (it may be said without exaggeration) very little educated, and having scarcely cultivated at all any of the higher faculties of mind. And in those countries the men who are acquainted with the principles of musical composition must be counted by hundreds, or more probably by thousands, the women barely by scores: so that here, again, on the doctrine of averages, we cannot reasonably expect to see more than one eminent woman to fifty eminent men; and the last three centuries have not produced fifty eminent male com· posers either in Germany or in Italy.

23. There are other reasons, besides those which we have now given, that help to explain why women remain behind men, even in the pursuits which are open to both. For one thing, very few women have time for them. This may seem a paradox; it is an undoubted social fact. The time and thoughts of every woman have to satisfy great previous demands on them for things practical. There is, first, the superintendence of the family and the domestic expenditure, which occupies at least one woman in every family, generally the one of mature years and acquired experience; unless the family is so rich as to admit of delegating that task to hired agency, and submitting to all the waste and malversation inseparable from that mode of conducting it. The superintendence of a household, even when not in other respects laborious, is extremely onerous to the thoughts; it requires incessant vigilance, an eye which no detail escapes, and presents questions for consideration and solution, foreseen and unforeseen, at every hour of the day, from which the person responsible for them can hardly ever shake herself free. If a woman is of a rank and circumstances which relieve her in a measure from these cares, she has still

devolving on her the management for the whole family of its whole intercourse with others—of what is called society—and the less the call made on her by the former duty, the greater is always the development of the latter: the dinner parties, concerts, evening parties, morning visits, letter-writing, and all that goes with them. All this is over and above the engrossing duty, which society imposes exclusively on women, of making themselves charming. A clever woman of the higher ranks finds nearly a sufficient employment of her talents in cultivating the graces of manner and the arts of conversation. To look only at the outward side of the subject: the great and continual exercise of thought which all women who attach any value to dressing well (I do not mean expensively, but with taste, and perception of natural and of artificial *convenance*) must bestow upon their own dress, perhaps also upon that of their daughters, would alone go a great way towards achieving respectable results in art, or science, or literature, and does actually exhaust much of the time and mental power they might have to spare for either.[1] If it were possible that all this number of little practical interests (which are made great to them) should leave them either much leisure, or much energy and freedom of mind, to be devoted to art or speculation, they must have a much greater original supply of active faculty than the vast majority of men. But this is not all. Independently of the regular offices of life which devolve upon a woman, she is expected to have her time and faculties always at the disposal of everybody. If a man has not a profession to exempt him from such demands, still, if he has a pursuit, he offends nobody by devoting his time to it; occupation is received as a valid excuse for his not answering to every casual demand which may be made on him. Are a woman's occupations, especially her chosen

[1] "It appears to be the same right turn of mind which enables a man to acquire the *truth*, or the just idea of what is right, in the ornaments, as in the more stable principles of art. It has still the same centre of perfection, though it is the centre of a smaller circle.—To illustrate this by the fashion of dress, in which there is allowed to be a good or bad taste. The component parts of dress are continually changing from great to little, from short to long; but the general form still remains: it is still the same general dress which is comparatively fixed, though on a very slender foundation; but it is on this which fashion must rest. He who invents with the most success, or dresses in the best taste, would probably, from the same sagacity employed to greater purposes, have discovered equal skill, or have formed the same correct taste, in the highest labours of art."—*Sir Joshua Reynolds' Discourses*, Disc. vii.

and voluntary ones, ever regarded as excusing her from any of
what are termed the calls of society? Scarcely are her most
necessary and recognized duties allowed as an exemption. It
requires an illness in the family, or something else out of the
common way, to entitle her to give her own business the prece-
dence over other people's amusement. She must always be at
the beck and call of somebody, generally of everybody. If she
has a study or a pursuit, she must snatch any short interval
which accidentally occurs to be employed in it. A celebrated
woman, in a work which I hope will some day be published, remarks truly that everything a woman does is done at odd times.
Is it wonderful, then, if she does not attain the highest eminence
in things which require consecutive attention, and the concentration on them of the chief interest of life? Such is philosophy,
and such, above all, is art, in which, besides the devotion of the
thoughts and feelings, the hand also must be kept in constant
exercise to attain high skill.

24. There is another consideration to be added to all these.
In the various arts and intellectual occupations, there is a
degree of proficiency sufficient for living by it, and there is
a higher degree on which depend the great productions which
immortalize a name. To the attainment of the former, there
are adequate motives in the case of all who follow the pursuit
professionally: the other is hardly ever attained where there is
not, or where there has not been at some period of life, an
ardent desire of celebrity. Nothing less is commonly a sufficient
stimulus to undergo the long and patient drudgery which, in
the case even of the greatest natural gifts, is absolutely required
for great eminence in pursuits in which we already possess so
many splendid memorials of the highest genius. Now, whether
the cause be natural or artificial, women seldom have this eager-
ness for fame. Their ambition is generally confined within
narrower bounds. The influence they seek is over those who
immediately surround them. Their desire is to be liked, loved,
or admired, by those whom they see with their eyes: and the
proficiency in knowledge, arts, and accomplishments, which
is sufficient for that, almost always contents them. This is
a trait of character which cannot be left out of the account in
judging of women as they are. I do not at all believe that it is
inherent in women. It is only the natural result of their circumstances. The love of fame in men is encouraged by education and opinion: to "scorn delights and live laborious days"

for its sake is accounted the part of "noble minds," even if spoken of as their "last infirmity," and is stimulated by the access which fame gives to all objects of ambition, including even the favour of women; while to women themselves all these objects are closed, and the desire of fame itself considered daring and unfeminine. Besides, how could it be that a woman's interests should not be all concentrated upon the impressions made on those who come into her daily life, when society has ordained that all her duties should be to them, and has contrived that all her comforts should depend on them? The natural desire of consideration from our fellow-creatures is as strong in a woman as in a man; but society has so ordered things that public consideration is, in all ordinary cases, only attainable by her through the consideration of her husband or of her male relations, while her private consideration is forfeited by making herself individually prominent, or appearing in any other character than that of an appendage to men.   Whoever is in the least capable of estimating the influence on the mind of the entire domestic and social position and the whole habit of a life, must easily recognize in that influence a complete explanation of nearly all the apparent differences between women and men, including the whole of those which imply any inferiority.

25. As for moral differences, considered as distinguished from intellectual, the distinction commonly drawn is to the advantage of women. They are declared to be better than men; an empty compliment, which must provoke a bitter smile from every woman of spirit, since there is no other situation in life in which it is the established order, and considered quite natural and suitable, that the better should obey the worse. If this piece of idle talk is good for anything, it is only as an admission by men of the corrupting influence of power; for that is certainly the only truth which the fact, if it be a fact, either proves or illustrates. And it *is* true that servitude, except when it actually brutalizes, though corrupting to both, is less so to the slaves than to the slave-masters. It is wholesomer for the moral nature to be restrained, even by arbitrary power, than to be allowed to exercise arbitrary power without restraint. Women, it is said, seldomer fall under the penal law—contribute a much smaller number of offenders to the criminal calendar—than men. I doubt not that the same thing may be said, with the same truth, of negro slaves. Those who are under the

control of others cannot often commit crimes, unless at the command and for the purposes of their masters. I do not know a more signal instance of the blindness with which the world, including the herd of studious men, ignore and pass over all the influences of social circumstances, than their silly depreciation of the intellectual, and silly panegyrics on the moral, nature of women.

26. The complimentary dictum about women's superior moral goodness may be allowed to pair off with the disparaging one respecting their greater liability to moral bias. Women, we are told, are not capable of resisting their personal partialities: their judgment in grave affairs is warped by their sympathies and antipathies. Assuming it to be so, it is still to be proved that women are oftener misled by their personal feelings than men by their personal interests. The chief difference would seem in that case to be, that men are led from the course of duty and the public interest by their regard for themselves, women (not being allowed to have private interests of their own) by their regard for somebody else. It is also to be considered, that all the education which women receive from society inculcates on them the feeling that the individuals connected with them are the only ones to whom they owe any duty—the only ones whose interest they are called upon to care for; while, as far as education is concerned, they are left strangers even to the elementary ideas which are presupposed in any intelligent regard for larger interests or higher moral objects. The complaint against them resolves itself merely into this, that they fulfil only too faithfully the sole duty which they are taught, and almost the only one which they are permitted to practise.

27. The concessions of the privileged to the unprivileged are so seldom brought about by any better motive than the power of the unprivileged to extort them, that any arguments against the prerogative of sex are likely to be little attended to by the generality, as long as they are able to say to themselves that women do not complain of it. That fact certainly enables men to retain the unjust privilege some time longer, but does not render it less unjust. Exactly the same thing may be said of the women in the harem of an Oriental: they do not complain of not being allowed the freedom of European women. They think our women insufferably bold and unfeminine. How rarely it is that even men complain of the general order

of society; and how much rarer still would such complaint be, if they did not know of any different order existing anywhere else. Women do not complain of the general lot of women; or rather they do, for plaintive elegies on it are very common in the writings of women, and were still more so as long as the lamentations could not be suspected of having any practical object. Their complaints are like the complaints which men make of the general unsatisfactoriness of human life; they are not meant to imply blame, or to plead for any change. But though women do not complain of the power of husbands, each complains of her own husband, or of the husbands of her friends. It is the same in all other cases of servitude, at least in the commencement of the emancipatory movement. The serfs did not at first complain of the power of their lords, but only of their tyranny. The commons began by claiming a few municipal privileges; they next asked an exemption for themselves from being taxed without their own consent; but they would at that time have thought it a great presumption to claim any share in the king's sovereign authority. The case of women is now the only case in which to rebel against established rules is still looked upon with the same eyes as was formerly a subject's claim to the right of rebelling against his king. A woman who joins in any movement which her husband disapproves makes herself a martyr, without even being able to be an apostle, for the husband can legally put a stop to her apostleship. Women cannot be expected to devote themselves to the emancipation of women, until men in considerable number are prepared to join with them in the undertaking.

CHAPTER IV

1. There remains a question, not of less importance than those already discussed, and which will be asked the most importunately by those opponents whose conviction is somewhat shaken on the main point. What good are we to expect from the changes proposed in our customs and institutions? Would mankind be at all better off if women were free? If not, why disturb their minds, and attempt to make a social revolution in the name of an abstract right?

2. It is hardly to be expected that this question will be asked

in respect to the change proposed in the condition of women in marriage. The sufferings, immoralities, evil of all sorts, produced in innumerable cases by the subjection of individual women to individual men, are far too terrible to be overlooked. Unthinking or uncandid persons, counting those cases alone which are extreme, or which attain publicity, may say that the evils are exceptional; but no one can be blind to their existence, nor, in many cases, to their intensity. And it is perfectly obvious that the abuse of the power cannot be very much checked while the power remains. It is a power given, or offered, not to good men, or to decently respectable men, but to all men; the most brutal, and the most criminal. There is no check but that of opinion, and such men are in general within the reach of no opinion but that of men like themselves. If such men did not brutally tyrannize over the one human being whom the law compels to bear everything from them, society must already have reached a paradisiacal state. There could be no need any longer of laws to curb men's vicious propensities. Astræa must not only have returned to earth, but the heart of the worst man must have become her temple. The law of servitude in marriage is a monstrous contradiction to all the principles of the modern world, and to all the experience through which those principles have been slowly and painfully worked out. It is the sole case, now that negro slavery has been abolished, in which a human being in the plenitude of every faculty is delivered up to the tender mercies of another human being, in the hope, forsooth, that this other will use the power solely for the good of the person subjected to it. Marriage is the only actual bondage known to our law. There remain no legal slaves, except the mistress of every house.

3. It is not, therefore, on this part of the subject that the question is likely to be asked, *Cui bono?* We may be told that the evil would outweigh the good, but the reality of the good admits of no dispute. In regard, however, to the larger question, the removal of women's disabilities—their recognition as the equals of men in all that belongs to citizenship—the opening to them of all honourable employments, and of the training and education which qualifies for those employments—there are many persons for whom it is not enough that the inequality has no just or legitimate defence; they require to be told what express advantage would be obtained by abolishing it.

4. To which let me first answer, the advantage of having the

most universal and pervading of all human relations regulated by justice instead of injustice. The vast amount of this gain to human nature, it is hardly possible, by any explanation or illustration, to place in a stronger light than it is placed by the bare statement, to anyone who attaches a moral meaning to words. All the selfish propensities, the self-worship, the unjust self-preference, which exists among mankind, have their source and root in, and derive their principal nourishment from, the present constitution of the relation between men and women. Think what it is to a boy, to grow up to manhood in the belief that, without any merit or any exertion of his own, though he may be the most frivolous and empty or the most ignorant and stolid of mankind, by the mere fact of being born a male he is by right the superior of all and every one of an entire half of the human race: including probably some whose real superiority to himself he has daily or hourly occasion to feel; but, even if in his whole conduct he habitually follows a woman's guidance, still, if he is a fool, he thinks that of course she is not, and cannot be, equal in ability and judgment to himself; and if he is not a fool, he does worse—he sees that she is superior to him, and believes that, notwithstanding her superiority, he is entitled to command and she is bound to obey. What must be the effect on his character of this lesson? And men of the cultivated classes are often not aware how deeply it sinks into the immense majority of male minds. For, among right-feeling and well-bred people, the inequality is kept as much as possible out of sight; above all, out of sight of the children. As much obedience is required from boys to their mother as to their father; they are not permitted to domineer over their sisters, nor are they accustomed to see these postponed to them, but the contrary; the compensations of the chivalrous feeling being made prominent, while the servitude which requires them is kept in the background. Well brought-up youths in the higher classes thus often escape the bad influences of the situation in their early years, and only experience them when, arrived at manhood, they fall under the dominion of facts as they really exist. Such people are little aware, when a boy is differently brought up, how early the notion of his inherent superiority to a girl arises in his mind; how it grows with his growth and strengthens with his strength; how it is inoculated by one schoolboy upon another; how early the youth thinks himself superior to his mother, owing her perhaps forbearance, but no real respect; and how sublime and sultan-like a sense of superiority he feels, above all, over the woman whom he honours by admitting her to a partnership of his life.   Is it imagined that all this does not pervert the whole manner of existence of the man, both as an individual and as a social being?   It is an exact parallel to the feeling of a hereditary king that he is excellent above others by being born a king, or a noble by being born a noble.   The relation between husband and wife is very like that between lord and vassal, except that the wife is held to more unlimited obedience than the vassal was.   However the vassal's character may have been affected, for better and for worse, by his subordination, who can help seeing that the lord's was affected greatly for the worse?— whether he was led to believe that his vassals were really superior to himself, or to feel that he was placed in command over people as good as himself, for no merits or labours of his own, but merely for having, as Figaro says, taken the trouble to be born.   The self-worship of the monarch, or of the feudal superior, is matched by the self-worship of the male. Human beings do not grow up from childhood in the possession of unearned distinctions without pluming themselves upon them. Those whom privileges not acquired by their merit, and which they feel to be disproportioned to it, inspire with additional humility, are always the few, and the best few.   The rest are only inspired with pride, and the worst sort of pride, that which values itself upon accidental advantages, not of its own achieving. Above all, when the feeling of being raised above the whole of the other sex is combined with personal authority over one in- dividual among them; the situation, if a school of conscientious and affectionate forbearance to those whose strongest points of character are conscience and affection, is to men of another quality a regularly constituted Academy or Gymnasium for training them in arrogance and overbearingness; which vices, if curbed by the certainty of resistance in their intercourse with other men, their equals, break out towards all who are in a position to be obliged to tolerate them, and often revenge themselves upon the unfortunate wife for the involuntary re- straint which they are obliged to submit to elsewhere.

5. The example afforded, and the education given to the sentiments, by laying the foundation of domestic existence upon a relation contradictory to the first principles of social justice, must, from the very nature of man, have a perverting influence

of such magnitude that it is hardly possible with our present experience to raise our imaginations to the conception of so great a change for the better as would be made by its removal. All that education and civilization are doing to efface the influences on character of the law of force, and replace them by those of justice, remains merely on the surface, as long as the citadel of the enemy is not attacked. The principle of the modern movement in morals and politics is that conduct, and conduct alone, entitles to respect: that not what men are, but what they do, constitutes their claim to deference; that, above all, merit, and not birth, is the only rightful claim to power and authority. If no authority, not in its nature temporary, were allowed to one human being over another, society would not be employed in building up propensities with one hand which it has to curb with the other. The child would really, for the first time in man's existence on earth, be trained in the way he should go, and when he was old there would be a chance that he would not depart from it. But so long as the right of the strong to power over the weak rules in the very heart of society, the attempt to make the equal right of the weak the principle of its outward actions will always be an uphill struggle; for the law of justice, which is also that of Christianity, will never get possession of men's inmost sentiments; they will be working against it, even when bending to it.

6. The second benefit to be expected from giving to women the free use of their faculties, by leaving them the free choice of their employments, and opening to them the same field of occupation and the same prizes and encouragements as to other human beings, would be that of doubling the mass of mental faculties available for the higher service of humanity. Where there is now one person qualified to benefit mankind and promote the general improvement, as a public teacher, or an administrator of some branch of public or social affairs, there would then be a chance of two. Mental superiority of any kind is at present everywhere so much below the demand; there is such a deficiency of persons competent to do excellently anything which it requires any considerable amount of ability to do; that the loss to the world, by refusing to make use of one-half of the whole quantity of talent it possesses, is extremely serious. It is true that this amount of mental power is not totally lost. Much of it is employed, and would in any case be employed, in domestic management,

and in a few other occupations open to women; and from the remainder indirect benefit is in many individual cases obtained, through the personal influence of individual women over individual men. But these benefits are partial; their range is extremely circumscribed; and if they must be admitted, on the one hand, as a deduction from the amount of fresh social power that would be acquired by giving freedom to one-half of the whole sum of human intellect, there must be added, on the other, the benefit of the stimulus that would be given to the intellect of men by the competition; or (to use a more true expression) by the necessity that would be imposed on them of deserving precedency before they could expect to obtain it.

7. This great accession to the intellectual power of the species, and to the amount of intellect available for the good management of its affairs, would be obtained, partly, through the better and more complete intellectual education of women, which would then improve pari passu with that of men. Women in general would be brought up equally capable of understanding business, public affairs, and the higher matters of speculation, with men in the same class of society; and the select few of the one as well as of the other sex, who were qualified not only to comprehend what is done or thought by others, but to think or do something considerable themselves, would meet with the same facilities for improving and training their capacities in the one sex as in the other. In this way, the widening of the sphere of action for women would operate for good, by raising their education to the level of that of men, and making the one participate in all improvements made in the other. But independently of this, the mere breaking down of the barrier would of itself have an educational virtue of the highest worth. The mere getting rid of the idea that all the wider subjects of thought and action, all the things which are of general and not solely of private interest, are men's business, from which women are to be warned off—positively interdicted from most of it, coldly tolerated in the little which is allowed them—the mere consciousness a woman would then have of being a human being like any other, entitled to choose her pursuits, urged or invited by the same inducements as anyone else to interest herself in whatever is interesting to human beings, entitled to exert the share of influence on all human concerns which belongs to an individual opinion, whether she attempted actual participation in them or not—this alone would effect an immense expansion

of the faculties of women, as well as enlargement of the range of their moral sentiments.

8. Besides the addition to the amount of individual talent available for the conduct of human affairs, which certainly are not at present so abundantly provided in that respect that they can afford to dispense with one-half of what nature proffers; the opinion of women would then possess a more beneficial, rather than a greater, influence upon the general mass of human belief and sentiment. I say a more beneficial, rather than a greater influence; for the influence of women over the general tone of opinion has always, or at least from the earliest known period, been very considerable. The influence of mothers on the early character of their sons, and the desire of young men to recommend themselves to young women, have in all recorded times been important agencies in the formation of character, and have determined some of the chief steps in the progress of civilization. Even in the Homeric age, αἰδώς towards the Τρωάδας ἑλκεσιπέπλους is an acknowledged and powerful motive of action in the great Hector. The moral influence of women has had two modes of operation. First, it has been a softening influence. Those who were most liable to be the victims of violence have naturally tended as much as they could towards limiting its sphere and mitigating its excesses. Those who were not taught to fight have naturally inclined in favour of any other mode of settling differences rather than that of fighting. In general, those who have been the greatest sufferers by the indulgence of selfish passion have been the most earnest supporters of any moral law which offered a means of bridling passion. Women were powerfully instrumental in inducing the northern conquerors to adopt the creed of Christianity, a creed so much more favourable to women than any that preceded it. The conversion of the Anglo-Saxons and of the Franks may be said to have been begun by the wives of Ethelbert and Clovis. The other mode in which the effect of women's opinion has been conspicuous, is by giving a powerful stimulus to those qualities in men which, not being themselves trained in, it was necessary for them that they should find in their protectors. Courage, and the military virtues generally, have at all times been greatly indebted to the desire which men felt of being admired by women: and the stimulus reaches far beyond this one class of eminent qualities, since, by a very natural effect of their position, the best passport to the admiration and favour of women has always been to be thought

highly of by men. From the combination of the two kinds of moral influence thus exercised by women, arose the spirit of chivalry: the peculiarity of which is, to aim at combining the highest standard of the warlike qualities with the cultivation of a totally different class of virtues—those of gentleness, generosity, and self-abnegation, towards the non-military and defenceless classes generally, and a special submission and worship directed towards women; who were distinguished from the other defenceless classes by the high rewards which they had it in their power voluntarily to bestow on those who endeavoured to earn their favour, instead of extorting their subjection. Though the practice of chivalry fell even more sadly short of its theoretic standard than practice generally falls below theory, it remains one of the most precious monuments of the moral history of our race; as a remarkable instance of a concerted and organized attempt, by a most disorganized and distracted society, to raise up and carry into practice a moral ideal greatly in advance of its social condition and institutions; so much so as to have been completely frustrated in the main object, yet never entirely inefficacious, and which has left a most sensible, and for the most part a highly valuable, impress on the ideas and feelings of all subsequent times.

9. The chivalrous ideal is the acme of the influence of women's sentiments on the moral cultivation of mankind: and if women are to remain in their subordinate situation, it were greatly to be lamented that the chivalrous standard should have passed away, for it is the only one at all capable of mitigating the demoralizing influences of that position. But the changes in the general state of the species rendered inevitable the substitution of a totally different ideal of morality for the chivalrous one. Chivalry was the attempt to infuse moral elements into a state of society in which everything depended for good or evil on individual prowess, under the softening influences of individual delicacy and generosity. In modern societies, all things, even in the military department of affairs, are decided, not by individual effort, but by the combined operations of numbers; while the main occupation of society has changed from fighting to business, from military to industrial life. The exigencies of the new life are no more exclusive of the virtues of generosity than those of the old, but it no longer entirely depends on them. The main foundations of the moral life of modern times must be justice and prudence; the respect of each for the rights of

every other, and the ability of each to take care of himself.
Chivalry left without legal check all forms of wrong which
reigned unpunished throughout society; it only encouraged a
few to do right in preference to wrong, by the direction it gave
to the instruments of praise and admiration. But the real
dependence of morality must always be upon its penal sanctions
—its power to deter from evil. The security of society cannot
rest on merely rendering honour to right, a motive so comparatively weak in all but a few, and which on very many does not
operate at all. Modern society is able to repress wrong through
all departments of life, by a fit exertion of the superior strength
which civilization has given it, and thus to render the existence
of the weaker members of society (no longer defenceless but
protected by law) tolerable to them, without reliance on the
chivalrous feelings of those who are in a position to tyrannize.
The beauties and graces of the chivalrous character are still
what they were, but the rights of the weak, and the general
comfort of human life, now rest on a far surer and steadier
support; or rather they do so in every relation of life except
the conjugal.

10. At present the moral influence of women is no less real,
but it is no longer of so marked and definite a character;
it has more nearly merged in the general influence of public
opinion. Both through the contagion of sympathy, and through
the desire of men to shine in the eyes of women, their feelings
have great effect in keeping alive what remains of the chivalrous ideal—in fostering the sentiments and continuing the
traditions of spirit and generosity. In these points of character,
their standard is higher than that of men; in the quality of
justice, somewhat lower. As regards the relations of private
life it may be said generally, that their influence is, on the
whole, encouraging to the softer virtues, discouraging to the
sterner ; though the statement must be taken with all the modifications dependent on individual character. In the chief of
the greater trials to which virtue is subject in the concerns
of life—the conflict between interest and principle—the tendency of women's influence is of a very mixed character. When
the principle involved happens to be one of the very few which
the course of their religious or moral education has strongly impressed upon themselves, they are potent auxiliaries to virtue: and
their husbands and sons are often prompted by them to acts of
abnegation which they never would have been capable of without that stimulus. But, with the present education and position

of women, the moral principles which have been impressed on them cover but a comparatively small part of the field of virtue, and are, moreover, principally negative; forbidding particular acts, but having little to do with the general direction of the thoughts and purposes. I am afraid it must be said that disinterestedness in the general conduct of life—the devotion of the energies to purposes which hold out no promise of private advantages to the family—is very seldom encouraged or supported by women's influence. It is small blame to them that they discourage objects of which they have not learnt to see the advantage, and which withdraw their men from them, and from the interests of the family. But the consequence is that woman's influence is often anything but favourable to public virtue.

11. Women have, however, some share of influence in giving the tone to public moralities since their sphere of action has been a little widened, and since a considerable number of them have occupied themselves practically in the promotion of objects reaching beyond their own family and household. The influence of women counts for a great deal in two of the most marked features of modern European life—its aversion to war, and its addiction to philanthropy. Excellent characteristics both; but unhappily, if the influence of women is valuable in the encouragement it gives to these feelings in general, in the particular applications the direction it gives to them is at least as often mischievous as useful. In the philanthropic department more particularly, the two provinces chiefly cultivated by women are religious proselytism and charity. Religious proselytism at home is but another word for embittering of religious animosities: abroad, it is usually a blind running at an object, without either knowing or heeding the fatal mischiefs—fatal to the religious object itself as well as to all other desirable objects—which may be produced by the means employed. As for charity, it is a matter in which the immediate effect on the persons directly concerned, and the ultimate consequence to the general good, are apt to be at complete war with one another: while the education given to women—an education of the sentiments rather than of the understanding—and the habit inculcated by their whole life, of looking to immediate effects on persons, and not to remote effects on classes of persons—make them both unable to see, and unwilling to admit, the ultimate evil tendency of any form of charity or philanthropy which commends itself to their sympathetic feelings. The great and continually increasing

mass of unenlightened and short-sighted benevolence, which, taking the care of people's lives out of their own hands, and relieving them from the disagreeable consequences of their own acts, saps the very foundations of the self-respect, self-help, and self-control which are the essential conditions both of individual prosperity and of social virtue—this waste of resources and of benevolent feelings in doing harm instead of good is immensely swelled by women's contributions, and stimulated by their influence.   Not that this is a mistake likely to be made by women, where they have actually the practical management of schemes of beneficence.   It sometimes happens that women who administer public charities—with that insight into present fact, and especially into the minds and feelings of those with whom they are in immediate contact, in which women generally excel men—recognize in the clearest manner the demoralizing influence of the alms given or the help afforded, and could give lessons on the subject to many a male political economist.   But women who only give their money, and are not brought face to face with the effects it produces, how can they be expected to foresee them ?   A woman born to the present lot of women, and content with it, how should she appreciate the value of self-dependence ?   She is not self-dependent; she is not taught self-dependence; her destiny is to receive everything from others, and why should what is good enough for her be bad for the poor? Her familiar notions of good are of blessings descending from a superior.   She forgets that she is not free, and that the poor are ; that if what they need is given to them unearned, they cannot be compelled to earn it ; that everybody cannot be taken care of by everybody, but there must be some motive to induce people to take care of themselves ; and that to be helped to help themselves, if they are physically capable of it, is the only charity which proves to be charity in the end.

12. These considerations show how usefully the part which women take in the formation of general opinion would be modified for the better by that more enlarged instruction, and practical conversancy with the things which their opinions influence, that would necessarily arise from their social and political emancipation.   But the improvement it would work through the influence they exercise, each in her own family, would be still more remarkable.

13. It is often said that, in the classes most exposed to temptation, a man's wife and children tend to keep him honest and respectable, both by the wife's direct influence, and by

the concern he feels for their future welfare. This may be
so, and no doubt often is so, with those who are more
weak than wicked; and this beneficial influence would be
preserved and strengthened under equal laws; it does not
depend on the woman's servitude, but is, on the contrary,
diminished by the disrespect which the inferior class of men
always at heart feel towards those who are subject to their
power. But when we ascend higher in the scale, we come
among a totally different set of moving forces. The wife's
influence tends, as far as it goes, to prevent the husband from
falling below the common standard of approbation of the
country. It tends quite as strongly to hinder him from rising
above it. The wife is the auxiliary of the common public
opinion. A man who is married to a woman his inferior in
intelligence, finds her a perpetual dead weight, or, worse than
a dead weight, a drag, upon every aspiration of his to be better
than public opinion requires him to be. It is hardly possible
for one who is in these bonds to attain exalted virtue. If he
differs in his opinion from the mass—if he sees truths which
have not yet dawned upon them, or if, feeling in his heart
truths which they nominally recognize, he would like to act up
to those truths more conscientiously than the generality of
mankind—to all such thoughts and desires marriage is the
heaviest of drawbacks, unless he be so fortunate as to have
a wife as much above the common level as he himself is.

14. For, in the first place, there is always some sacrifice of
personal interest required; either of social consequence, or of
pecuniary means; perhaps the risk of even the means of subsistence. These sacrifices and risks he may be willing to en-
counter for himself; but he will pause before he imposes them
on his family. And his family in this case means his wife and
daughters; for he always hopes that his sons will feel as he
feels himself, and that what he can do without, they will do
without, willingly, in the same cause. But his daughters—their
marriage may depend upon it: and his wife, who is unable
to enter into or understand the objects for which these
sacrifices are made—who, if she thought them worth any
sacrifice, would think so on trust, and solely for his sake—
who could participate in none of the enthusiasm or the
self-approbation he himself may feel, while the things
which he is disposed to sacrifice are all in all to her; will
not the best and most unselfish man hesitate the longest
before bringing on her this consequence? If it be not

the comforts of life, but only social consideration that is at
stake, the burthen upon his conscience and feelings is still very
severe. Whoever has a wife and children has given hostages
to Mrs. Grundy. The approbation of that potentate may be a
matter of indifference to him, but it is of great importance to
his wife. The man himself may be above opinion, or may find
sufficient compensation in the opinion of those of his own way
of thinking. But to the women connected with him, he can
offer no compensation. The almost invariable tendency of the
wife, to place her influence in the same scale with social consideration, is sometimes made a reproach to women, and repre-
sented as a peculiar trait of feebleness and childishness of
character in them: surely with great injustice. Society makes
the whole life of a woman, in the easy classes, a continued self-
sacrifice; it exacts from her an unremitting restraint of the
whole of her natural inclinations, and the sole return it makes
to her for what often deserves the name of a martyrdom is
consideration. Her consideration is inseparably connected with
that of her husband, and after paying the full price for it, she
finds that she is to lose it, for no reason of which she can feel
the cogency. She has sacrificed her whole life to it, and her
husband will not sacrifice to it a whim, a freak, an eccentricity;
something not recognized or allowed for by the world, and
which the world will agree with her in thinking a folly, if it
thinks no worse! The dilemma is hardest upon that very
meritorious class of men, who, without possessing talents which
qualify them to make a figure among those with whom they
agree in opinion, hold their opinion from conviction, and feel
bound in honour and conscience to serve it, by making profession of their belief, and giving their time, labour, and means,
to anything undertaken in its behalf. The worst case of all is
when such men happen to be of a rank and position which of
itself neither gives them, nor excludes them from, what is
considered the best society; when their admission to it depends mainly on what is thought of them personally—and,
however unexceptionable their breeding and habits, their being
identified with opinions and public conduct unacceptable to
those who give the tone to society would operate as an effectual
exclusion. Many a woman flatters herself (nine times out of ten
quite erroneously) that nothing prevents her and her husband
from moving in the highest society of her neighbourhood—
society in which others well known to her, and in the same
class of life, mix freely—except that her husband is un-

fortunately a Dissenter, or has the reputation of mingling in low radical politics. That it is, she thinks, which hinders George from getting a commission or a place, Caroline from making an advantageous match, and prevents her and her husband from obtaining invitations, perhaps honours, which, for aught she sees, they are as well entitled to as some folks. With such an influence in every house, either exerted actively or operating all the more powerfully for not being asserted, is it any wonder that people in general are kept down in that mediocrity of respectability which is becoming a marked characteristic of modern times?

15. There is another very injurious aspect in which the effect, not of women's disabilities directly, but of the broad line of difference which those disabilities create between the education and character of a woman and that of a man, requires to be considered. Nothing can be more unfavourable to that union of thoughts and inclinations which is the ideal of married life. Intimate society between people radically dissimilar to one another is an idle dream. Unlikeness may attract, but it is likeness which retains; and in proportion to the likeness is the suitability of the individuals to give each other a happy life. While women are so unlike men, it is not wonderful that selfish men should feel the need of arbitrary power in their own hands, to arrest *in limine* the lifelong conflict of inclinations, by deciding every question on the side of their own preference. When people are extremely unlike, there can be no real identity of interest. Very often there is conscientious difference of opinion between married people, on the highest points of duty. Is there any reality in the marriage union where this takes place? Yet it is not uncommon anywhere, when the woman has any earnestness of character; and it is a very general case indeed in Catholic countries, when she is supported in her dissent by the only other authority to which she is taught to bow, the priest. With the usual barefacedness of power not accustomed to find itself disputed, the influence of priests over women is attacked by Protestant and Liberal writers, less for being bad in itself, than because it is a rival authority to the husband, and raises up a revolt against his infallibility. In England, similar differences occasionally exist when an Evangelical wife has allied herself with a husband of a different quality; but in general this source at least of dissension is got rid of, by reducing the minds of women to such a nullity that they have no opinions but those of Mrs. Grundy, or those which the husband

tells them to have. When there is no difference of opinion, differences merely of taste may be sufficient to detract greatly from the happiness of married life. And, though it may stimulate the amatory propensities of men, it does not conduce to married happiness, to exaggerate by differences of education whatever may be the native differences of the sexes. If the married pair are well-bred and well-behaved people, they tolerate each other's tastes; but is mutual toleration what people look forward to, when they enter into marriage? These differences of inclination will naturally make their wishes different, if not restrained by affection or duty, as to almost all domestic questions which arise. What a difference there must be in the society which the two persons will wish to frequent, or be frequented by! Each will desire associates who share their own tastes: the persons agreeable to one will be indifferent or positively disagreeable to the other; yet there can be none who are not common to both, for married people do not now live in different parts of the house and have totally different visiting lists, as in the reign of Louis XV. They cannot help having different wishes as to the bringing up of the children : each will wish to see reproduced in them their own tastes and sentiments; and there is either a compromise, and only a half-satisfaction to either, or the wife has to yield—often with bitter suffering; and, with or without intention, her occult influence continues to counterwork the husband's purposes.

16. It would of course be extreme folly to suppose that these differences of feeling and inclination only exist because women are brought up differently from men, and that there would not be differences of taste under any imaginable circumstances. But there is nothing beyond the mark in saying that the distinction in bringing-up immensely aggravates those differences, and renders them wholly inevitable. While women are brought up as they are, a man and a woman will but rarely find in one another real agreement of tastes and wishes as to daily life. They will generally have to give it up as hopeless, and renounce the attempt to have, in the intimate associate of their daily life, that *idem velle, idem nolle*, which is the recognized bond of any society that is really such : or if the man succeeds in obtaining it, he does so by choosing a woman who is so complete a nullity that she has no *velle* or *nolle* at all, and is as ready to comply with one thing as another if anybody tells her to do so. Even this calculation is apt to fail; dullness and want of spirit are not always a guarantee of the submission

which is so confidently expected from them. But if they were,
is this the ideal of marriage? What, in this case, does the man
obtain by it, except an upper servant, a nurse, or a mistress?
On the contrary, when each of two persons, instead of being a
nothing, is a something; when they are attached to one another,
and are not too much unlike to begin with; the constant par-
taking in the same things, assisted by their sympathy, draws out
the latent capacities of each for being interested in the things
which were at first interesting only to the other; and works a
gradual assimilation of the tastes and characters to one another,
partly by the insensible modification of each, but more by a real
enriching of the two natures, each acquiring the tastes and
capacities of the other in addition to its own. This often
happens between two friends of the same sex, who are much
associated in their daily life; and it would be a common, if not
the commonest, case in marriage, did not the totally different
bringing-up of the two sexes make it next to an impossibility to
form a really well-assorted union. Were this remedied, whatever differences there might still be in individual tastes, there
would at least be, as a general rule, complete unity and unanimity as to the great objects of life. When the two persons
both care for great objects, and are a help and encouragement
to each other in whatever regards these, the minor matters on
which their tastes may differ are not all-important to them; and
there is a foundation for solid friendship, of an enduring character, more likely than anything else to make it, through the
whole of life, a greater pleasure to each to give pleasure to the
other than to receive it.

17. I have considered, thus far, the effects on the pleasures
and benefits of the marriage union which depend on the mere
unlikeness between the wife and the husband: but the evil
tendency is prodigiously aggravated when the unlikeness is inferiority. Mere unlikeness, when it only means difference of
good qualities, may be more a benefit, in the way of mutual
improvement, than a drawback from comfort. When each
emulates, and desires and endeavours to acquire, the other's
peculiar qualities, the difference does not produce diversity of
interest, but increased identity of it, and makes each still more
valuable to the other. But when one is much the inferior of the
two in mental ability and cultivation, and is not actively attempting by the other's aid to rise to the other's level, the whole influence of the connection upon the development of the superior
of the two is deteriorating: and still more so in a tolerably happy

marriage than in an unhappy one. It is not with impunity that the superior in intellect shuts himself up with an inferior, and elects that inferior for his chosen, and sole completely intimate, associate. Any society which is not improving is deteriorating: and the more so, the closer and more familiar it is. Even a really superior man almost always begins to deteriorate when he is habitually (as the phrase is) king of his company: and in his most habitual company the husband who has a wife inferior to him is always so. While his self-satisfaction is incessantly ministered to on the one hand, on the other he insensibly imbibes the modes of feeling, and of looking at things, which belong to a more vulgar or a more limited mind than his own. This evil differs from many of those which have hitherto been dwelt on, by being an increasing one. The association of men with women in daily life is much closer and more complete than it ever was before. Men's life is more domestic. Formerly, their pleasures and chosen occupations were among men, and in men's company; their wives had but a fragment of their lives. At the present time, the progress of civilization, and the turn of opinion against the rough amusements and convivial excesses which formerly occupied most men in their hours of relaxation—together with (it must be said) the improved tone of modern feeling as to the reciprocity of duty which binds the husband towards the wife—have thrown the man very much more upon home and its inmates, for his personal and social pleasures: while the kind and degree of improvement which has been made in women's education, has made them in some degree capable of being his companions in ideas and mental taste, while leaving them, in most cases, still hopelessly inferior to him. His desire of mental communion is thus in general satisfied by a communion from which he learns nothing. An unimproving and unstimulating companionship is substituted for (what he might otherwise have been obliged to seek) the society of his equals in powers and his fellows in the higher pursuits. We see, accordingly, that young men of the greatest promise generally cease to improve as soon as they marry, and, not improving, inevitably degenerate. If the wife does not push the husband forward, she always holds him back. He ceases to care for what she does not care for; he no longer desires, and ends by disliking and shunning, society congenial to his former aspirations, and which would now shame his falling off from them; his higher faculties both of mind and heart cease to be called into activity. And, this change coincid-

ing with the new and selfish interests which are created by the
family, after a few years he differs in no material respect from
those who have never had wishes for anything but the common
varieties and the common pecuniary objects.

18. What marriage may be in the case of two persons of
cultivated faculties, identical in opinions and purposes, between
whom there exists that best kind of equality, similarity of
powers and capacities with reciprocal superiority in them—
so that each can enjoy the luxury of looking up to the other,
and can have alternately the pleasure of leading and of being led
in the path of development—I will not attempt to describe. To
those who can conceive it, there is no need; to those who
cannot, it would appear the dream of an enthusiast. But I
maintain, with the profoundest conviction, that this, and this
only, is the ideal of marriage; and that all opinions, customs,
and institutions which favour any other notion of it, or turn the
conceptions and aspirations connected with it into any other
direction, by whatever pretences they may be coloured, are
relics of primitive barbarism. The moral regeneration of mankind will only really commence, when the most fundamental
of the social relations is placed under the rule of equal justice,
and when human beings learn to cultivate their strongest
sympathy with an equal in rights and in cultivation.

19. Thus far, the benefits which it has appeared that the
world would gain by ceasing to make sex a disqualification for
privileges and a badge of subjection, are social rather than
individual; consisting in an increase of the general fund of
thinking and acting power, and an improvement in the general
conditions of the association of men with women. But it would
be a grievous understatement of the case to omit the most direct
benefit of all, the unspeakable gain in private happiness to the
liberated half of the species; the difference to them between a
life of subjection to the will of others, and a life of rational
freedom. After the primary necessities of food and raiment,
freedom is the first and strongest want of human nature.
While mankind are lawless, their desire is for lawless freedom.
When they have learnt to understand the meaning of duty and
the value of reason, they incline more and more to be guided
and restrained by these in the exercise of their freedom; but
they do not therefore desire freedom less; they do not become
disposed to accept the will of other people as the representative
and interpreter of those guiding principles. On the contrary,
the communities in which the reason has been most cultivated,

and in which the idea of social duty has been most powerful, are those which have most strongly asserted the freedom of action of the individual—the liberty of each to govern his conduct by his own feelings of duty, and by such laws and social restraints as his own conscience can subscribe to.

20. He who would rightly appreciate the worth of personal independence as an element of happiness, should consider the value he himself puts upon it as an ingredient of his own. There is no subject on which there is a greater habitual difference of judgment between a man judging for himself and the same man judging for other people. When he hears others complaining that they are not allowed freedom of action—that their own will has not sufficient influence in the regulation of their affairs—his inclination is to ask, what are their grievances? what positive damage they sustain? and in what respect they consider their affairs to be mismanaged? And if they fail to make out, in answer to these questions, what appears to him a sufficient case, he turns a deaf ear, and regards their complaint as the fanciful querulousness of people whom nothing reasonable will satisfy. But he has a quite different standard of judgment when he is deciding for himself. Then, the most unexceptionable administration of his interests by a tutor set over him does not satisfy his feelings: his personal exclusion from the deciding authority appears itself the greatest grievance of all, rendering it superfluous even to enter into the question of mismanagement. It is the same with nations. What citizen of a free country would listen to any offers of good and skilful administration, in return for the abdication of freedom? Even if he could believe that good and skilful administration can exist among a people ruled by a will not their own, would not the consciousness of working out their own destiny under their own moral responsibility be a compensation to his feelings for great rudeness and imperfection in the details of public affairs? Let him rest assured that whatever he feels on this point, women feel in a fully equal degree. Whatever has been said or written, from the time of Herodotus to the present, of the ennobling influence of free government—the nerve and spring which it gives to all the faculties, the larger and higher objects which it presents to the intellect and feelings, the more unselfish public spirit, and calmer and broader views of duty, that it engenders, and the generally loftier platform on which it elevates the individual as a moral, spiritual, and social being—is every particle as true of women as of men. Are these things no important part

of individual happiness? Let any man call to mind what he himself felt on emerging from boyhood—from the tutelage and control of even loved and affectionate elders—and entering upon the responsibilities of manhood. Was it not like the physical effect of taking off a heavy weight, or releasing him from obstructive, even if not otherwise painful, bonds? Did he not feel twice as much alive, twice as much a human being, as before? And does he imagine that women have none of these feelings? But it is a striking fact that the satisfactions and mortifications of personal pride, though all in all to most men when the case is their own, have less allowance made for them in the case of other people, and are less listened to as a ground or a justification of conduct, than any other natural human feelings; perhaps because men compliment them in their own case with the names of so many other qualities, that they are seldom conscious how mighty an influence these feelings exercise in their own lives. No less large and powerful is their part, we may assure ourselves, in the lives and feelings of women. Women are schooled into suppressing them in their most natural and most healthy direction, but the internal principle remains, in a different outward form. An active and energetic mind, if denied liberty, will seek for power: refused the command of itself, it will assert its personality by attempting to control others. To allow to any human beings no existence of their own but what depends on others, is giving far too high a premium on bending others to their purposes. Where liberty cannot be hoped for, and power can, power becomes the grand object of human desire; those to whom others will not leave the undisturbed management of their own affairs, will compensate themselves, if they can, by meddling for their own purposes with the affairs of others. Hence also women's passion for personal beauty, and dress and display; and all the evils that flow from it, in the way of mischievous luxury and social immorality. The love of power and the love of liberty are in eternal antagonism. Where there is least liberty, the passion for power is the most ardent and unscrupulous. The desire of power over others can only cease to be a depraving agency among mankind, when each of them individually is able to do without it: which can only be where respect for liberty in the personal concerns of each is an established principle.

21. But it is not only through the sentiment of personal dignity that the free direction and disposal of their own faculties is a source of individual happiness, and to be fettered and

restricted in it a source of unhappiness, to human beings, and
not least to women.   There is nothing, after disease, indigence,
and guilt, so fatal to the pleasurable enjoyment of life as the
want of a worthy outlet for the active faculties.   Women who
have the cares of a family, and while they have the cares of a
family, have this outlet, and it generally suffices for them: but
what of the greatly increasing number of women who have had
no opportunity of exercising the vocation which they are mocked
by telling them is their proper one?   What of the women whose
children have been lost to them by death or distance, or have
grown up, married, and formed homes of their own?   There are
abundant examples of men who, after a life engrossed by business, retire with a competency to the enjoyment, as they hope,
of rest, but to whom, as they are unable to acquire new interests
and excitements that can replace the old, the change to a life
of inactivity brings ennui, melancholy, and premature death.
Yet no one thinks of the parallel case of so many worthy
and devoted women, who, having paid what they are told is
their debt to society—having brought up a family blamelessly
to manhood and womanhood—having kept a house as long
as they had a house needing to be kept—are deserted by the
sole occupation for which they have fitted themselves; and
remain with undiminished activity but with no employment for
it, unless perhaps a daughter or daughter-in-law is willing to
abdicate in their favour the discharge of the same functions in
her younger household.   Surely a hard lot for the old age of
those who have worthily discharged, as long as it was given to
them to discharge, what the world accounts their only social
duty.   Of such women, and of those others to whom this duty
has not been committed at all—many of whom pine through
life with the consciousness of thwarted vocations, and activities
which are not suffered to expand—the only resources, speaking
generally, are religion and charity.   But their religion, though
it may be one of feeling, and of ceremonial observance, cannot
be a religion of action, unless in the form of charity.   For
charity many of them are by nature admirably fitted; but to
practise it usefully, or even without doing mischief, requires
the education, the manifold preparation, the knowledge and
the thinking powers, of a skilful administrator.   There are
few of the administrative functions of government for which
a person would not be fit, who is fit to bestow charity usefully.   In this as in other cases (pre-eminently in that of
the education of children), the duties permitted to women

cannot be performed properly, without their being trained for duties which, to the great loss of society, are not permitted to them. And here let me notice the singular way in which the question of women's disabilities is frequently presented to view, by those who find it easier to draw a ludicrous picture of what they do not like than to answer the arguments for it. When it is suggested that women's executive capacities and prudent counsels might sometimes be found valuable in affairs of state, these lovers of fun hold up to the ridicule of the world, as sitting in parliament or in the cabinet, girls in their teens, or young wives of two or three and twenty, transported bodily, exactly as they are, from the drawing-room to the House of Commons. They forget that males are not usually selected at this early age for a seat in Parliament, or for responsible political functions. Common sense would tell them that if such trusts were confided to women, it would be to such as, having no special vocation for married life, or preferring another employment of their faculties (as many women even now prefer to marriage some of the few honourable occupations within their reach), have spent the best years of their youth in attempting to qualify themselves for the pursuits in which they desire to engage; or still more frequently perhaps widows or wives of forty or fifty, by whom the knowledge of life and faculty of government which they have acquired in their families could, by the aid of appropriate studies, be made available on a less contracted scale. There is no country of Europe in which the ablest men have not frequently experienced, and keenly appreciated, the value of the advice and help of clever and experienced women of the world, in the attainment both of private and of public objects; and there are important matters of public administration to which few men are equally competent with such women; among others, the detailed control of expenditure. But what we are now discussing is not the need which society has of the services of women in public business, but the dull and hopeless life to which it so often condemns them, by forbidding them to exercise the practical abilities which many of them are conscious of, in any wider field than one which to some of them never was, and to others is no longer, open. If there is anything vitally important to the happiness of human beings, it is that they should relish their habitual pursuit. This requisite of an enjoyable life is very imperfectly granted, or altogether denied, to a large part of mankind; and by its absence many a life is a failure, which is provided in appearance with every requisite of success. But if circumstances, which society is not yet skilful enough to overcome, render such failures often for the present inevitable, society need not inflict them. The injudiciousness of parents, a youth's own inexperience, or the absence of external opportunities for the congenial vocation, and their presence for an uncongenial, condemn numbers of men to pass their lives in doing one thing reluctantly and ill, when there are other things which they could have done well and happily. But on women this sentence is imposed by actual law, and by customs equivalent to law. What, in unenlightened societies, colour, race, religion, or, in the case of a conquered country, nationality, are to some men, sex is to all women; a peremptory exclusion from almost all honourable occupations, but either such as cannot be fulfilled by others, or such as those others do not think worthy of their acceptance. Sufferings arising from causes of this nature usually meet with so little sympathy, that few persons are aware of the great amount of unhappiness even now produced by the feeling of a wasted life. The case will be even more frequent as increased cultivation creates a greater and greater disproportion between the ideas and faculties of women and the scope which society allows to their activity.

22. When we consider the positive evil caused to the disqualified half of the human race by their disqualification—first in the loss of the most inspiriting and elevating kind of personal enjoyment, and next in the weariness, disappointment, and profound dissatisfaction with life, which are so often the substitute for it—one feels that, among all the lessons which men require for carrying on the struggle against the inevitable imperfections of their lot on earth, there is no lesson which they more need than not to add to the evils which nature inflicts, by their jealous and prejudiced restrictions on one another. Their vain fears only substitute other and worse evils for those which they are idly apprehensive of: while every restraint on the freedom of conduct of any of their human fellow-creatures (otherwise than by making them responsible for any evil actually caused by it) dries up *pro tanto* the principal fountain of human happiness, and leaves the species less rich, to an inappreciable degree, in all that makes life valuable to the individual human being.

OTHER BOOKS BY
FREDERICK ELLIS

Author - Jack London

MARTIN EDEN

WAR OF THE CLASSES

JOHN BARLEYCORN

THE PEOPLE OF THE ABYSS

JACK LONDON ON THE ROAD

THE ASSASSINATION BUREAU, LTD.

THE IRON HEEL

Author – B. Traven

GENERAL FROM THE JUNGLE

THE DEATH SHIP

THE REBELLION OF THE HANGED

THE WHITE ROSE

THE BRIDGE IN THE JUNGLE

MARCH TO THE MONTERIA

THE TREASURE OF THE SIERRA MADRE

> Author - Carl Frederick

est PLAYING THE GAME THE NEW WAY

> Authors - Frederick Ellis & Carl Frederick

THE OAKLAND STATEMENT

> Author – Mao Tsetung

QUOTATIONS FROM CHAIRMAN MAO TSETUNG

> Author – Upton Sinclair

OUR LADY

THE FLIVVER KING: THE STORY OF FORD-AMERICA

ONE HUNDRED PERCENT: THE STORY OF A PATRIOT

WORLD'S END I

WORLD'S END II

THE SECRET LIFE OF JESUS

THE MONEYCHANGERS

MENTAL RADIO

THE MILLENNIUM

A PERSONAL JESUS

PROFITS OF RELIGION

THEY CALL ME CARPENTER: A TALE OF
THE SECOND COMING

Author – Thomas Paine

COMMON SENSE, THE RIGHTS OF MAN
& THE AGE OF REASON

THE AMERICAN CRISIS

Author – Karl Marx

DAS KAPITAL

THE COMMUNIST MANIFESTO &
WAGES, PRICE AND PROFIT

WAGE-LABOUR AND CAPITAL
& VALUE. PRICE AND PROFIT

Author – Eugene Debs

WALLS AND BARS

Author – Jean-Jacques Rousseau

THE SOCIAL CONTRACT

Author – John Reed

TEN DAYS THAT SHOOK THE WORLD

INSURGENT MEXICO

Author – Antonio Gramsci

**THE MODERN PRINCE AND
SELECTED WRITINGS**

Author – V. I. Lenin

THE STATE AND REVOLUTION

**FIGHT AGAINST STALINISM & IMPERIALISM:
THE HIGHEST STAGE OF CAPITALISM**

Author – David Ricardo

**PRINCIPLES OF POLITICAL ECONOMY
AND TAXATION**

Author – Thomas Jefferson

**BIOGRAPHY OF THOMAS JEFFERSON & THE
LIFE AND MORALS OF JESUS OF NAZARETH**

Author – Emma Goldman

ANARCHISM AND OTHER WRITINGS

www.ingramcontent.com/pod-product-compliance
Lightning Source LLC
Chambersburg PA
CBHW021535260326
41914CB00001B/30